Unseen

A fresh look at the spirit world and how we can protect ourselves from the devil's schemes

Written by

Tom Rawls

Published by Tom Rawls
In association with Awesome House Productions

Copyright © 2018 Bobby Thomas Rawls

ISBN: - 9781-7941-0571-3

All rights reserved. No part of this publication may be reproduced or transmitted in any form or by any means, electronic or mechanical including photocopying, recording or any information storage or retrieval system, without prior permission in writing from the publisher. For permission contact the author by email: tomrawls@proclaimers.com

The right of Bobby Thomas Rawls (also known as Tom Rawls) to be identified as the author of this work has been asserted by him in accordance with the copyright, Design and Patents Act of 1988

First Published by Awesome House production in the United Kingdom in 2018

Unless otherwise stated, all scripture quotations are taken from the Holy Bible, New International Version. Copyright © 1954, 1958, 1962, 1965, 1987 by the Lockman Foundation

MSG - The Message Copyright © 1993, 1994, 1995, 1996, 2000, 2001, 2002, by Eugene H. Peterson

NKJV - The Holy Bible, New King James Version Copyright © 1982 by Thomas Nelson Inc

KJV - The Holy Bible, King James Version Public domain

TPT - Scripture quotations marked TPT are from The Passion Translation®. Copyright © 2017, 2018 by Passion & Fire Ministries, Inc. Used by permission. All rights reserved. ThePassionTranslation.com.

These versions are also referenced:

NIVUK - Holy Bible, New International Version® Anglicized, NIV® Copyright © 1979, 1984, 2011 by **Biblica, Inc®** Used by permission. All rights reserved worldwide.

NCV - Scripture taken from the New Century Version®. Copyright © 2005 by Thomas Nelson. Used by permission. All rights reserved.

NLT - HOLY BIBLE, New Living Translation, copyright © 1996, 2004, 2015 by Tyndale House Foundation. Used by permission of Tyndale House Publishers, Inc., Carol Stream, Illinois 60188. All rights reserved.

JB Philips - The New Testament in Modern English by J.B Phillips copyright © 1960, 1972 J. B. Phillips. Administered by The Archbishops' Council of the Church of England. Used by permission.

Cover art created by Scott McCrum and Sam Cousins. The figure on the front cover is a chimera from the Notre Dame of Paris. This figure watches out over Paris. Much of the church's religious imagery was destroyed in the 1790s during the French Revolution. In 1845, Architect Eugene Violet-le-Duc began extensive restoration to the cathedral, returning it to its original Gothic state. Violet-le-Duc also added the chimeras. This particular chimera is called "The Hyena."

To Denise, my partner in crime, travel companion and my sweetheart forever.

To Rebekah, I'm so proud of who you've become. Serve God with a full heart.

To Daniel, love you in every way. Keep desiring God and His calling on your life.

You are all people of destiny!

What are people saying about Tom Rawls and his previous books?

Brian Houston, Global Founder and Senior Pastor of Hillsong Church. *Tom's broad life-experiences, coupled with his service to the Church have given him a unique perspective and understanding. I believe those who venture into these pages will see the Church from a more vibrant perspective - as profoundly powerful and vastly underestimated.*

Craig Groeschel, Senior Pastor of *LifeChurch.tv*, *Tom Rawls' passion for the local Church and all that it can accomplish is inspiring. This is a good book for anyone who needs reminding of the beauty, power and true mission of God's Church.*

Mal Fletcher, Chairman of 2020Plus, social commentator, broadcaster, futurist and author. *In Relentless, Tom Rawls gives us a compelling vision of the majestic force Christ's Church might become, if she is willing to re-align herself with the revolutionary principles of the New Testament. His call for leadership over management and spiritual potency over fatalistic defeatism, must not fall on deaf ears if Western Church is to once more become Christ's 'city on a hill'.*

Dave Gilpin, Senior Pastor of Hope City Church, England and author of a runaway seller *Sacred Cows Make Great BBQs.* *'Relentless' has always been the tattoo etched into the heart of Tom Rawls. In the eighties he broke tradition and touched a youth culture for Jesus, in the nineties he touched the world's underclass, and this century he is touching the Western world for Jesus. He has never relinquished, never quit, never backed down and never stopped. This book is infectious. You may become what you read.*

Wayne alcorn, president of the australian christian churches and senior pastor of Brisbane city church, australia. *Tom rawls is a pioneer. He's a "journey man", and he's been used by god to provoke thought and action. It has been an inspiration to watch him lead in his own unique style for almost 3 decades in 3 very different cultures (australia, thailand and the uk). All the while, he has retained a freshness in his approach to leadership, a passion to stay in touch with culture and a prophetic edge to his message. This book captures his quest for truth and relevance, his understanding of current trends, and his heart to see the church be the unstoppable force its founder meant it to be.*

'Relentless' and 'Plain View' by Tom Rawls are available on Amazon Kindle.
'Plain View' is also available in print through Amazon or www.proclaimers.com

Contents

Introduction: An understanding of the spirit world

Chapter 1. Folk – Fusion twists on Christian Theology

Chapter 2. The opening verses of Ephesians 6: 10 – 13

Chapter 3. The belt of truth

Chapter 4. The breastplate of righteousness

Chapter 5. Feet fitted with the gospel of peace

Chapter 6. The shield of faith

Chapter 7. The helmet of salvation

Chapter 8. The sword of the Spirit

Chapter 9. Pray in the Spirit

Epilogue

Introduction:
An understanding of the spirit world

"There are two equal and opposite errors into which our race can fall about the devils. One is to disbelieve in their existence. The other is to believe, and to feel an excessive and unhealthy interest in them."
C.S. Lewis, "The Screwtape Letters"

"Demons were like genies or philosophy professors if you didn't word things exactly right, they delighted in giving you absolutely accurate and completely misleading answers."
Sir Terence David John Pratchett OBE

The Lord said to Satan, "Where have you come from?" Satan answered the Lord, "From roaming throughout the earth, going back and forth on it."
Job 1:7

Many people are totally unaware of the spirit realm. The problem is you can't see it with your natural eyes. The spirit realm, according to scripture, is inhabited by God, angels and demons. The spirit realm is a hidden state, an unseen country and is thoroughly concealed from our human senses. We simply can't see it, but if we ignore it, we do so at our own risk.

Scripture teaches us that there is an interaction between the seen and unseen realm. The Bible's teachings indicate that God loves us and seeks to interact with us through His word, the Bible, and through our prayers. His world is a spiritual world, and His interactions are for our good. God at times employs the use of His angels to help and minister to us. **Hebrews 1:14** states, "Are not all angels ministering spirits sent to serve those who will inherit salvation?"

But there is also a dark unseen world. I wish to speak about this realm and how it impacts our lives and how we can protect ourselves from the vicious and spiteful attacks that come upon us from this evil realm.

In the dark unseen world, there is a malevolent personality reigning over it. He is the Devil. What truly matters is this unseen empire can have a direct and targeted impact on our world, on our lives and on the many challenges we face day to day. Disregarding or overlooking the truth of this dark domain will result in danger to our eternal soul. How do we protect ourselves from the schemes of hell?

Bureaucracy and the dark unseen realm.
The Bible goes to lengths to explain to us the degree of organisation present in both the world we see and in the world we cannot see. Paul writes in **Colossians 1:16**, speaking of Christ, "For in him all things were created: things in heaven and on earth, *visible and invisible*, whether thrones or powers or rulers or authorities; all things have been created through him and for him."

Notice the designations; "thrones, powers, rulers and authorities." Our political world, which we observe in society, is built upon layer over layer of bureaucracy and it certainly impacts our lives. In the same way, the spirit realm has layers and levels that affect us as well. As Paul describes they are *invisible* thrones, powers, rulers and authorities. Most people are unaware and ignorant of these invisible powers; but Paul is manifestly clear these things exist and can have a deadly impact upon our lives.

The fact that scripture describes these invisible powers is... what can I say... astonishing!

The description of the spirit world is quite profound for us as western people. I mean most of us have a theology of the Devil and of evil spirits, but we are reluctant to explore too deeply that theology for fear of being labelled fanatical, weird or super spiritual. Mostly we feel it is not scientific enough to garner real energy to think it through. To be honest it is a bit of a dark study and mostly an undesirable discipline to consider.

Unlike the western Christian mind, other world cultures have a rich tapestry of invisible "spirits" that require sacrifice, appeasement and recognition. To the 21st Century rational mind, especially in the west, we find this all a bit fanciful, far-fetched and bizarre. Other cultures, though, have fantastical stories, legends and folklore to describe it all and they do so in extraordinary detail.

Western Christians have less of an interest and in turn less understanding of this unseen world and its impact upon our lives. Other cultures though have developed systems to rank and define their understanding of the spirit world. We in the west tend to lump it all together as just demons, and we'd rather not talk about it, or conversely, we talk about it way too much for it to be healthy.

One of our great authors of the 20th century drew attention to this realm in his now classic book "The Screwtape Letters." Clive Staples Lewis, who died 22 November 1963, was a British novelist, poet, academic, literary critic, essayist, lay theologian, broadcaster, lecturer, and Christian apologist. He is best known for his works of fiction, especially "The Screwtape Letters" and "The Chronicles of Narnia" and for his non-fiction Christian apologetics, such as "Mere Christianity," and "The Problem of Pain." C.S. Lewis and fellow novelist J. R. R. Tolkien were close friends.

"The Screwtape Letters" was first published in February 1942, the story takes the form of a series of letters from a senior demon named Screwtape to his nephew a Junior Tempter named Wormwood. The uncle's mentorship pertains to the nephew's responsibility in securing the damnation of a British man known only as "the Patient". God is referred to as "The Enemy", as you would expect. The book is insightful as to how demons interact against us from the spirit realm. It has insights into how God works and most would say this is an apologetic wrapped around a work of fiction. It is none the less an interesting use of C.S. Lewis imagination and genius as an author. It was dedicated to J.R.R. Tolkien. I have highlighted his work by quoting from "The Screwtape Letters" at the beginning of each chapter.

Throughout scripture, the authors of both the New and Old Testaments mention the existence of many gods and goddess. The Bible gives accounts of the sacrifices these demon gods required, the pageantry they needed and the passion with which people worshipped and served these gods. Far from saying they didn't exist the scripture said they were a real and present danger to the souls of those who worshipped or interacted with them. Idolatry is of course prohibited under God's law for His people the Jews; there was a reason for this prohibition!

Lucifer.
The scriptures tell a remarkable story of an angelic being called Lucifer. Lucifer was one of the archangels created by God in Heaven before time began on Earth. Lucifer, at some time after his creation, rebelled against God, in turn, desired to be like God and to claim God's throne. The scriptures explain how Lucifer instigated a rebellion in Heaven which resulted in himself and a third of the "angels" being cast out. Lucifer became Satan, and the third of the angels cast out of heaven became the demons of the dark world under Satan's control.

Note this amazing Bible reference: **Ezekiel 28: 12 – 15,** speaking of Lucifer, "You were the seal of perfection, full of wisdom and perfect in beauty. You were in Eden, the garden of God; every precious stone adorned you: carnelian, chrysolite and emerald, topaz, onyx and jasper, lapis lazuli, turquoise and beryl. Your settings and mountings were made of gold; on the day you were created they were prepared. You were anointed as a guardian cherub, for so I ordained you. You were on the holy mount of God; you walked among the fiery stones. You were blameless in your ways from the day you were created till wickedness was found in you."

Lucifer, after his expulsion from heaven, became known as Satan, the adversary. His other designations are the god of this world, the devil, Beelzebub, the prince of the power of the air. Isaiah calls him the Day-Star, Paul speaks of him as an angel of light, Peter speaks of him as being like a roaring lion. But there is no doubt that Lucifer or Satan is the prince of a dark domain and is its nefarious, dark lord.

Have a look at this passage from the Prophet **Isaiah 14: 11 – 17**, "All your pomp has been brought down to the grave, along with the noise of your harps; maggots are spread out beneath you and worms cover you. How you have fallen from heaven, morning star, son of the dawn! You have been cast down to the earth, you who once laid low the nations! You said in your heart, "I will ascend to the heavens; I will raise my throne above the stars of God; I will sit enthroned on the mount of assembly, on the utmost heights of Mount Zaphon. I will ascend above the tops of the clouds; I will make myself like the Most High." But you are brought down to the realm of the dead, to the depths of the pit. Those who see you stare at you, they ponder your fate: "Is this the man who shook the earth and made kingdoms tremble, the man who made the world a wilderness, who overthrew its cities and would not let his captives go home?""

Pride fuelled Lucifer's rebellion against God. Five times Lucifer boasted "I will" ending with his greatest blasphemy, "I will make myself like the Most High." It was his pride and his determination to be like God that resulted in him being "brought down to the realm of the dead, to the depths of the pit." His proud exclamations resulting in his ultimate expulsion was followed by his utter humiliation at the hands of God. At the genesis of human history, Lucifer appears again and **Genesis 3** records a compelling and vivid account of him as an ancient serpent who brought down the human race inciting them to rebellion against God command. His greatest temptation to Eve? Eat this fruit, and you will be like God! (Genesis 3:5)

Making our way in the unseen realm.
So how do we navigate this invisible world? How do we fight what we cannot see? How do we win the battles against these spirit beings so set on our destruction? How do we face the challenges of a spirit world which is imperceptible to our five senses? Thankfully the Bible gives us a clear picture.

Paul the Apostle put it this way in **Ephesians 6: 10 – 13**. "Finally, be strong in the Lord and in his mighty power. Put on the full armour of God, so that you can take your stand against the devil's schemes. For our struggle is not against flesh and blood, but against the rulers, against the authorities, against the powers of this dark world and against the spiritual forces of evil in the heavenly realms. Therefore put on the full armour of God, so that when the day of evil comes, you may be able to stand your ground, and after you have done everything, to stand."

God's protective gear for our earthly struggles.
Paul speaks and teaches us about **"The Armour of God."** In a recent series of messages in our church Proclaimers, I opened up these passages of scripture to our congregation. I felt my messages were fresh, potent and even more relevant to us today than they had been ever before. I knew then this preaching series would be a book and a teaching guide to equip churches, church leaders and Christians for the challenges life throws our way.

I desired to present a series that would help us to comprehend these truths *sanely and biblically*. I want the teachings of this book to be a guiding principle as we wrestle against the powers of this dark world.

Now remember this is an epic struggle. Without sounding too alarming or fanatical, this is an existential threat to every person alive on the planet today. So as a desire, I want everyone who reads this book, Christian or non-Christian, to have available a resource to help them to win in this battle.

Just a few thoughts to ponder.
- Because of sin we live in a fallen world groaning for the day of redemption.[1]
- Satan, the great Beast, has been judged but not yet confined to eternal punishment.[2]
- This ancient serpent is presently the god (little "g") of this world[3]
- Satan roams around like a roaring lion seeking someone to devour.[4]
- The Devil and his army of dark lords hate the human race because we bear the image of God.[5]
- The Devil's desire and stated goal is to destroy that image and make it unrecognisable to God.
- The destruction of humanity, this is Satan's revenge on God for being shunned and cast out of Heaven.

[1] Romans 8:22

[2] John 16:11

[3] 2 Corinthians 4:4

[4] 1 Peter 5:8

[5] John 10:10

Satan wants to destroy us!
Yes, it is true; there is a battle going on in the world today. It is a battle of heroic proportions, and it is mostly invisible and unseen by the five senses of a human's experience. But just because it is invisible does not mean it is no less real. This is our struggle. But God has not left us unprotected from these unseen being. In fact, the armour He provides, which also exists in the unseen realm, is hardy, robust and tough and will withstand any and every attack from our unseen foes.

So buckle your seatbelts for a fresh look at the armour God has given us. Get ready for a sane, balanced and reasonable explanation to "spiritual warfare." Find truth that won't make you look and sound stupid to a waiting world, who themselves are desperate for a way out of their brokenness and darkness. Find help in your wrestle against beings who are more powerful than us, hidden from our natural senses and have had millennium to hone their psychological skills to defeat us, undermine us, deceive us and destroy us.

From scripture and in the pages of my book find out how God has prepared a way for us to "stand our ground" against the dark forces of this world. In this book, I offer a theology and a strategy to stand strong when the "day of evil" comes your way.

I hope you enjoy this book and the study into Paul's words found in Ephesians chapter 6.

Tom Rawls
Norwich, England
August 2018
tomrawls@proclaimers.com

Chapter 1
A folk-fusion twist on Christian Theology

"The truth is that the Enemy, having oddly destined these mere animals to life in His own eternal world, has guarded them pretty effectively from the danger of feeling at home anywhere else. That is why we must often wish long life to our patients; seventy years is not a day too much for the difficult task of unravelling their souls from Heaven and building up a firm attachment to the earth. While they are young, we find them always shooting off at a tangent."
C.S. Lewis, "The Screwtape Letters"

"Demons are like obedient dogs; they come when they are called."
Rémy de Gourmont
French Symbolist poet, novelist, and influential critic

"The God of peace will swiftly pound Satan to a pulp under your feet! And the wonderful favor of our Lord Jesus will surround you."
Romans 16:20 TPT

I worked and lived with my wife and kids in Bangkok, Thailand for over 12 years. I travelled the region extensively, including some time in Dhaka, Bangladesh. During that time I studied Buddhism, Islam and the folk-fusion variations of both. The folk-fusion side tended to be more about evil and helpful spirits, occult and magic than either religion would endorse in its strictest form. The studies were interesting and helped me relate my Christian faith in both spheres as I sought to share the salvation message of Jesus to the world I lived and worked in.

Folk-fusion is not a new kind of music or international cuisine. It's a mishmash of religious customs and practices that are outside the official doctrine and practices of the religion. For example, the Islam practised in Bangladesh would be looked down upon by visiting Saudis as being impure and blasphemous. So much of Bangladeshi Islam relies upon the activity of evil spirits and occult practices.

Just as the Buddhism practised in Thailand would be looked down upon by a practising student of Zen. The religions in these countries are a mishmash of different beliefs. Just like there are Asian Fusion restaurants that have dabbled in mixing up their menu items, so there is a folk-fusion in most major religions of the world. For example, in Thailand, I've seen candles and incense being burned for Mary the mother of Jesus in front of a Catholic church. The fusion of religious customs is rife in many countries.

I have discovered there is also a "Christian" version of folk-fusion beliefs as well. I know it may sound strange to say this, but I find there are some who teach, as truth, things only based upon their experience rather than what the scriptures actually say. **Chris Caine,** an evangelist (and a lot more to the body of Christ) once tweeted, *"If you don't know what God really said, you will fall for what anybody says."* Sage advice.

It concerns me when people base their theology and practices on experience or based on a book or sermon someone once preached rather than scripture. There is no research, no going to the Bible to search for truth. Their information comes to them in an oral history of what someone once experienced rather than the principles of scripture. When this happens, their version of truth is merely anecdotal and subjective. They draw down on passages of scripture, take them out of context and use them as proof texts to back up their experiences and practices. It concerns me because these customs and practices are taught as being biblical when in fact they are not. It makes us look and sound foolish.

One such practice I have seen is the practice of "spiritual warfare." Let me tell you a story.

In my time as a missionary in Thailand, a group of "prayer warriors" came to Bangkok. They asked to meet with me before their task at hand, hoping for a bit of advice concerning culture, and a few do's and don'ts. I was happy to oblige. They told me they were here in Bangkok to do a "prayer walk" to find out what the major and dominant spiritual powers over the city were. They said they wanted to find out so they could then conduct "spiritual warfare" and pray against these demon powers to see a revival in the city of Bangkok. They were very sincere people. And let's face it, Bangkok could do with a lot of prayers!

To help them in their search of what the dominant spirits over Bangkok are I told them the Thais had already discovered this information and had named five major spirits as the ruling spirits over the city. I told them I could take them to the place where these demons "lived." The place is called Lak Muang or City Pillars where there are enshrined the five demons, or as the Thais call them, "Angels."

I felt like I had disappointed the group somewhat as it appeared they wanted to "prayer walk" around Bangkok and find this information out for themselves rather than rely upon the research of those who had lived in Bangkok for decades. They wanted the Holy Spirit to reveal this information to them. So they decided to not go to the Lak Muang instead they would just "prayer walk." It is a pity they refused the trip to Lak Muang as it would have simplified their work immensely!

After a few days of walking around Bangkok, they informed me that their revelation from God was that the main spirit over our city was a spirit of "Lust." Bangkok is, of course, a main centre in Asia for the sex trade, sex trafficking and all manner of immorality. I could have told them this information quite quickly with no prayer involved at all. But they maintained this is what the Holy Spirit had revealed, and so they committed themselves to "spiritual warfare" and prayed against the spirit of lust.

They told me they would first name the spirit and then "bind" the spirit. They said they prayed for about 3 days until they felt they had substantially weakened the spirit. They prayed another few days and then informed me the spirit had been suitably bound in Jesus Name! The "stronghold" had been broken. They prophesied that we would see major revival over the city breaking out from today.

The next day they jumped on their planes and went back to their country. Needless to say, the sex trade in Bangkok is still flourishing. Thankfully the work of the Lord in Thailand continues to grow and expand. Was their "spiritual warfare" a factor in this? Maybe, I'm not sure. There is no objective evidence to substantiate this. My question is what did they actually do? Was their activity and actions supported by scripture? I'm sure their prayers for Bangkok helped, but I am less sure that what they did was scripturally informed.

Spiritual Warfare.
Let me state for the record, I believe in spiritual warfare. The scriptures speak plainly and unmistakably of evil spirits, demons, and clearly, these malevolent spirits mean us no good. The scriptures clearly teach that Jesus cast out evil spirits from people. His disciples did likewise. In Ephesians 6, Paul is clear we 'armour up' so we can stand in the day of evil. But is standing our ground the same as "spiritual warfare?"

There is a reference to spiritual warfare and it is in heaven and found in Daniel when the archangels fight against the prince of Persia and the prince of Greece. There is a fascinating account in **Jude 1:9** of Michael the archangel not being willing to bring an accusation of slander against the Devil but said, "The Lord rebuke you." There is another reference in Revelation when, once again, the archangel fights against Satan and throws him into the pit of fire and brimstone.

In Paul's writings, there is mention of our weapons of war not being of the flesh. Meaning they are not flesh and blood weapons. Our weapons exist in the unseen realm as does our enemy. Unseen – not easily recognised by our five human senses.

2 Corinthians 10: 3 – 6 says, "For though we live in the world, we do not wage war as the world does. The weapons we fight with are not the weapons of the world. On the contrary, they have divine power to demolish strongholds. We demolish arguments and every pretension that sets itself up against the knowledge of God, and we take captive every thought to make it obedient to Christ. And we will be ready to punish every act of disobedience, once your obedience is complete."

This passage says we have weapons "not of this world" and that we do not wage war as the world does. So what are our weapons of war? How do we wage war?

Examples of folk-fusion practices:
What is the ministry of deliverance? For some, they feel they have a ministry whereby they can cast out evil spirits from people. Jesus cast our spirits. Paul did. The disciples of Jesus did but had limited success in this area. The words of **William Cowper,** English poet and Hymn writer, are true when he says "Satan trembles when he sees the weakest saint upon their knees." I believe the Bible teaches we all have authority over evil spirits in Jesus' name. I don't believe the Bible teaches there is a specific ministry of deliverance instead every saint has authority over all the power of the enemy.

So can a person have a demon inside of them? Absolutely! Does that demon control them? Yes, it does, to varying degrees. Can a servant of Jesus cast out that demon? Again, absolutely! It's when we turn our eyes away from the risen Christ and become distracted by demons that we seem to see more demons than we see of Jesus.

There are quite a few books written about the subject of casting out demons. In my early days as a Christian, I was subjected to deliverance prayers repeatedly. Looking back now I wonder, how did so many evil spirits get into me and why did it take so many months to be set free from them? I put it down now to a limited understanding of scripture and erroneous teaching. I was young and unschooled in scripture and theology. I think we deal with this subject today differently because of a greater understanding of Jesus and a greater understanding of our salvation.

Jesus said in **Luke 10: 19 - 20**, "I have given you authority to trample on snakes and scorpions and to overcome all the power of the enemy; nothing will harm you. *However, do not rejoice that the spirits submit to you, but rejoice that your names are written in heaven.*"

The focus of our attention is crucial. Keep your eyes on salvation and the power of that Good News not on whether demons are subject to you. For instance, I've been in a meeting where the worship leader would say, "I sense an oppressive spirit here this morning." Some in the audience would begin muttering the name of Jesus. The worship leader would then commence to "bind" the spirit in Jesus name. Apparently, the atmosphere would lift, and the worship would continue. I find this kind of practice to be a combination of fusion–folk religious practices and a misguided understanding of scripture. The problem is, it sounds very spiritual, but I'm concerned by the emphasis.

I've heard people when they pray "claim the blood of Jesus." I know this sounds spiritual too, but there is no mention of us "claiming the blood of Jesus" anywhere in scripture. This phrase is not part of a magical formula for defeating demons. Now, do not hear what I'm not saying. The subject of the blood of Jesus is paramount to our salvation. But when scripture speaks about the precious blood of Jesus, the writers are mostly speaking in terms of the substitutional death and resurrection of Jesus, individually that Jesus bled and died for us, not of 'claiming the blood of Jesus'.

1 Peter 1: 18 – 19 says we were redeemed by the precious blood of Jesus but quickly goes on to say "a lamb without blemish or defect." Again the picture being painted for anyone with an association with animal sacrifices would understand the power of the blood being shed for the forgiveness of our sins. The pleading of the blood as some would claim is not the scriptural term but a folk-fusion custom.

People have visited my house at times and comment on some of my South East Asian artefacts. They are beautiful, and each purchase has memories and stories of my time spent in those foreign lands. One of my purchases were bought in China Town in Bangkok. I found these wooden Chinese letters which in Chinese mean "Health, Prosperity and Long Life." These wooden letters were actual Chinese words. I really appreciated the message behind each word.

One day someone came into my house and stated rather aggressively that they were demonic. I quietly explained that these are merely Chinese words (letters that carry meaning) how can they be demonic? She said she "felt" they were of the devil. My next question floored her. I asked then is the whole Chinese alphabet demonic as well as these letters? #embarrassed

Some people tend to see demons everywhere. They have an unhealthy obsession. Like one person who commented on my tie. They said the elephants in the weave were demonic! It goes on! People get a "sense" that this or that is demonic. It becomes their theology and their special ministry to discern what things are demonic or not. I think this practice is misguided. It is an out of focus perspective. There is no biblical premise upon which we can state an elephant is demonic.

One man who was staying the night in our home commented he was uncomfortable with a book in his room which he referred to as a book about "blood sucking Vampires!" He said he didn't sleep well because of it. It was a book my daughter had borrowed from a friend called "Twilight." I said I'd remove the book from his room and hoped he would sleep better the next night! This 'demon discerning' is folk-fusion religious belief with no biblical borders. It's a bit like holding out a cross to protect yourself from an advancing vampire. (Don't panic-I know that vampires don't exist LOL)

I had someone in my house who commented on a book by Ernest Hemmingway, "A Moveable Feast." The book is a memoir by the American author about his years as a struggling young expatriate journalist and writer in Paris in the 1920s. It's a thin book I've read maybe 10 times! Usually on the plane as I fly to Paris. It was difficult to have a great conversation with this gentleman because he went on to criticise another book on my shelf which was the biography of Sigmund Freud. I mentioned that Hemmingway was a Pulitzer Prize winning journalist and Freud one of the most significant and influential voices in understanding the human mind. He was not convinced!

This same man voiced concerns over to me for playing Beethoven at dinner time saying he didn't like Beethoven because he was "... a very very angry man." I said politely, "You know he was deaf in a day and age when people didn't understand these kinds of disabilities. No wonder he was angry."

To change the subject, I asked who he would like to listen too. He mentioned Mozart, (who by the way was a drunkard and a womaniser) or Tchaikovsky (who suffered from depression and had syphilis). Now I love both Mozart and Tchaikovsky. So we played them for him. But where is it found that Beethoven is demonic and Tchaikovsky is ok? Again, I like them both. There is no objective proof that these classic musicians are demonic. Instead, it is a folk-fusion response to things we've heard about these musicians and interpret them as being satanic. Some people live in fear, not faith.

What do people actually believe and is it biblical? Do their beliefs have any scriptural context or backing? Do people not know who they are in Christ? Where does this kind of teaching come from? Do we have authority over the Devil or not?

Just for fun. **Franz Alexander von Kleist**, a German poet from the 1800's, once said about Mozart, "Mozart's music is so beautiful as to entice angels down to earth." **Georg Solti** Hungarian born conductor once commented, "Mozart makes you believe in God because it cannot be by chance that such a phenomenon arrives into this world and leaves such an unbounded number of unparalleled masterpieces."

Finally, **Karl Barth,** renowned Swiss Reformed Theologian, once said, "It may be that when the angels go about their task praising God, they play only Bach. I am sure, however, that when they are together en famille, they play Mozart." I like Mozart's music. I also appreciate Beethoven and Tchaikovsky as well as George Benson, Miles Davis, John Coltrane. I like a lot of music. I don't live in fear of Satan thinking he can secretly influence my life by listening to Beethoven or John Coltrane.

Does anyone remember back in the early 80's when we were instructed by our youth leaders to burn our vinyl? Because if you played the record backwards, there was a subliminal message from the Devil. I burned dozens of albums. Thankfully, I have managed to build up a rather impressive collection again.

I had a young man in my church who was a university student and came from a black church in London. He said that over summer their church prayed and fasted for 40 days. I was impressed but asked why? He said to break hereditary or generational curses. I was a bit taken back and shocked. Here I am thinking that Jesus covered that in our redemption! I suppose they might have lost a bit of weight and did spend some extra time in prayer which was good. But how do we find a theology of breaking the generational curse when Jesus in the resurrection broke every curse over our lives as part of our great and glorious salvation?

Galatians 3:13 TPT says it this way, "Yet, Christ paid the full price to set us free from the curse of the law. He absorbed it completely as he became a curse in our place. For it is written: Everyone who is hung upon a tree is doubly cursed." Christ paid the full price to set us free!

Where do people get these kinds of teaching? In the midst of folk-fusion teaching of Christian themes, we find a lot of people writing on the subject of demons, and it concerns me the imbalance of the teaching. To me, their teaching puts way too much emphasis on the Devil and distracts us from the foundation truths of scripture concerning salvation, redemption, the resurrection and the believer's authority in the now ascended Christ.

Jesus said in **Luke 10:20**, "... do not rejoice that the spirits submit to you, but rejoice that your names are written in heaven." The subject of focus is essential.

The struggle is real.
The scripture does tell us there is a struggle going on in the unseen world, the spirit world. There is no doubt, the struggle is real! Paul declares our wrestle is not against humans, not "flesh and blood" but our wrestle is against demonic powers of various kinds. We all know humans play a part in our struggles but the *source* of our struggles are not human but spiritual, and Paul was going to give us instructions on how to protect ourselves and stand strong when the evil days come upon us. Our response was not to be only flesh and blood, but spiritual as well.

It's vital for us to know that in **Ephesians 6** Paul is not teaching that we are struggling *for* victory – instead, the emphasis of the passage is we wrestle *from* victory. It's still a wrestle, a struggle and a battle but we do it from the standpoint of Christ has already won the victory, and we fight in it, not for it.

In the Passion Translation the translator puts it this way: **Ephesians 6:10**, "Now my beloved ones, I have saved these most important truths for last: Be supernaturally infused with strength through your life-union with the Lord Jesus. Stand victorious with the force of his explosive power flowing in and through you."

Be supernaturally infused with strength, to me, this is a direct link to the power we know through the baptism in the Holy Spirit. This Holy Spirit power is an essential part of our Christian lives that Jesus insisted we experience before we started out on our journey to win the world for Him. It was a vital thing we needed to experience as the church before we were to be His witnesses throughout the world.

This strength Paul speaks of comes to us because of our union with Jesus. Christ in us, our hope of glory! This strength we've receive is through our salvation and our faith in the risen Lord Jesus. He gives us the power to "stand victorious" with the force of His explosive power flowing in us and through us! Wow – this sounds like a confident and victorious life we live against our enemy.

Let me continue with the Passion Translation of these verses; **Ephesians 6: 11 – 13**, "Put on God's complete set of armour provided for us, so that you will be protected as you fight against the evil strategies of the accuser! Your hand-to-hand combat is not with human beings, but with the highest principalities and authorities operating in rebellion under the heavenly realms. For they are a powerful class of demon-gods and evil spirits that hold this dark world in bondage. Because of this, you must wear all the armour that God provides so you're protected as you confront the slanderer, for you are destined for all things and will rise victorious."

We are all aware there is a struggle associated with life. Trials and tribulations, troubles and struggles – it's all a part of life – no secrete there! But it is not a struggle for victory but a struggle from victory. Paul speaks metaphorically about the armour that is available for our ongoing protection. This armour God provides is for protection so that we "will rise victorious" in all our struggles. It's an amazing turn of phrase here. We wrestle – there is a struggle – there is "hand to hand combat with powerful demon gods" but we will emerge from this combat and will rise victorious. We may be knocked down, but not out, if we heed the instructions of scripture.

As we navigate our lives, we are reminded we live and operate in a fallen world. This world is also under the influence of Satan. **2 Corinthians 4:4** refers to him as the "god of this world." The very phrase "god of this world" (or "god of this age") indicates that Satan is a significant influence on the ideals, opinions, goals, hopes and views of the majority of people. His influence, which is spiritual, also impacts the world's governments, philosophies, education, and commerce. These thoughts, ideas and speculations are influenced by him and have sprung up from his lies and deceptions.

In this world we will experience trouble, says Jesus and we all know that to be true. We know and understand life will be complicated by strife, sickness, stress and suffering but we continue on knowing that this kind of trouble produces within us maturity.

In life, we will wrestle and struggle, and if we understand the power of God and the protections He has given us, we will find ourselves rising to victory, not wallowing in defeat. Jesus is promising us victory in the midst of turmoil. We can stand in the evil day, and we can experience victory against the forces of evil. He overcame the world, and He gives us the power to do the same.

Jesus gives us the victory over all of the powers of hell. We have this victory by expressing our faith in the power of His salvation purchased for us by His precious blood. We've been saved by Jesus and rescued from the dominion of the devil. This is biblical truth. This is our salvation.

Chapter 2
The opening verses of Ephesians 6: 10 – 13

"Do not be deceived, Wormwood. Our cause is never more in danger than when a human, no longer desiring, but intending, to do our Enemy's will, looks round upon a universe from which every trace of Him seems to have vanished, and asks why he has been forsaken, and still obeys."
C.S. Lewis "The Screwtape Letters."

"Demons wait at crossroads attempting to influence our decisions."
April Smith
An American folk rock/indie pop singer

Since all his "children" have flesh and blood, so Jesus became human to fully identify with us. He did this, so that he could experience death and annihilate the effects of the intimidating accuser who holds against us the power of death.
Hebrews 2:14 TPT

My first few years of ministry were extremely tough. I was a pioneer pastor. I went out and started churches from scratch. The first church I started was in Alice Springs – the centre of Australia. It is an isolated part of our great country of Australia being right in the heart of the nation surrounded by deserts. There is still a significant church today, 40 years on.

It was a tough 3 years! It was my baptism of fire. I was only 22, really young and really lacking in maturity. But I had a go for Jesus. It was in Alice I experienced two of the three death threats made on my life, just because I had stirred up the Devil and rattled his cage so badly! It was a tough time, but **I found myself up for the challenge.**

I was working to some extent in a cross-cultural setting as well as reaching out to and at times working with aboriginal communities. I became aware of some of their ancient beliefs. I saw first-hand how a normal, healthy young man wasted away in an Alice Springs hospital simply because one of the head men had "pointed the bone" at him. He eventually died in hospital. Doctors were confounded by what he died from.

I heard and saw many manifestations of demon activity while living in Alice Springs. It was fascinating and a big learning curve for me. I found out about aboriginal culture, I discovered some knowledge of "Dream Time" teachings and was privy to knowledge of the feared Kurdaitcha Man. Aboriginal culture describes the Kurdaitcha Man as a ritual executioner. It is said the shoes worn by the Kurdaitcha Man were woven of emu feathers and human hair and treated with blood. It is said he could vanish into thin air. He only travels at night and is known to have great knowledge and supernatural power.

The teaching of the "Dream Time" is about the Australian Aboriginal's understanding of the world, of its creation, and its great stories. It is a supernatural account of all kinds of spirit beings and their interactions upon the world as they know it. It is intricate, elaborate and a sophisticated way of looking at their world.

In my ministry in the Northern Territory, I travelled all over and had many exciting cultural and spiritual experiences. It was a tough time, many challenges and trying times – but it was a remarkable time of learning. Alice Springs was a beautiful town, and it was a great season in my life. Surrounded by deserts and some of the most dramatic landscape anyone would want to see yet……. What was I doing that caused so much trouble? Why were the powers of darkness giving me such a hard time?

Paul the Apostle wrote the Epistle of the Ephesians in, or around, 62AD while he was imprisoned in Rome. His chapter 6 would have been written in an atmosphere of imminent death and possible torture. It was written in a day when Paul was threatened by death daily and the powers of Rome encroaching upon his freedoms. His guards were Roman soldiers and, I am sure, in the midst of his imprisonment he got great inspiration from their armour.

He wrote in **Ephesians 6: 10 – 13** "Finally, be strong in the Lord and in his mighty power. Put on the full armour of God, so that you can take your stand against the devil's schemes. For our struggle is not against flesh and blood, but against the rulers, against the authorities, against the powers of this dark world and against the spiritual forces of evil in the heavenly realms. Therefore put on the full armour of God, so that when the day of evil comes, you may be able to stand your ground, and after you have done everything, to stand."

This letter was written to the church in Ephesus. It is important to know that Ephesus was home to the most worshipped God in all of the world. Her fame was indeed world-wide. She was the goddess Diana. A Temple was constructed to house her image. She is portrayed as having many breasts as a sign of her fertility. This temple dominated the religious, cultural and economic scene of the city. The city of Ephesus was the centre of Diana's worship and hence the governing authorities were responsible for maintaining her temple as part of their municipal duties.

The temple of Diana was also called the Temple of Artemis. Hundreds of eunuch priests and religious prostitutes served the goddess. The rituals, performed daily were erotic and highly sexualised. The worship of Diana brought much fame and tourism to the city, so much so, that Ephesus is regarded as having one of the largest banks in Asia. It was to this city that Paul wrote his letter. A city infested with demon powers and occult practices. It was in this atmosphere that the great Ephesian church flourished. The church was led by Paul's son in the faith Timothy. Historians suggest the church numbered over 60,000 people. It was in this hellhole, dominated by the powers of darkness that Paul writes to us to put on God's armour so we can stand against the powers of evil.

Many people are blind to the real source of their challenges. Many are ignorant of our enemies schemes perpetrated against us. Many people misidentify the origin of their struggles. It looks so much like flesh and blood! It's a miscalculation on our part when we treat these kinds of challenges as *merely* a flesh and blood experience when in fact the Bible says the source is far more sinister.

Yet some, knowing and recognising the source, still fight in a manner that actually misdirects their energies and depletes their strength. They fight in a way that gets them off course and entirely distracted from God's plans. They fight "like a boxer beating the air." They lack a biblical strategy, and as a result, waste time and energy.

Some become "super spirituals" who look for demons in every corner and under every rock. They have an unhealthy obsession with demons and lose focus in the fight. Like the TV exorcists who use a Bible or a cross when encouraging the demons to come out of the subject. What's worse the anecdotal recount of their experience becomes solid "theology" for others. It's true; this kind of misguided experience has launched many books, ministries and some bizarre practices. I sincerely hope mine can be different.

NOTE: *Paul is quite clear, our struggles are not merely against "flesh and blood."* Our struggles find their origins in the spirit world. I know this may sound bizarre – but Paul teaches that the source of our challenges is spiritual. Be encouraged though – the answer to our struggles is also found in the spirit realm! It may look like flesh and blood, but the origin is spiritual. To navigate the natural, we will need wisdom and insight. Dealing with people is essential, but to win the battle we will need a spiritual focus to our perspective.

NOTE: Paul does not tell us to fight the devil and his angels but instead to be strong in the Lord. This is all about focus and perspective. Paul teaches us to **"Be strong in the Lord and in his mighty power."** For those living in resurrection life and steeped in biblical truth, we know the enemy has already been defeated, and we actually have victory over him. When Jesus rose again from the dead, He overcame Satan, Hell and Death leaving us with a complete and comprehensive victory over them all. We don't wrestle for victory we wrestle from victory.

Being strong in the Lord also speaks to us as maturing believers. Believers who have sought to live lives worthy of the name of Jesus. Believers who seek after holiness and living a life without a hint of immoral behaviour. Being strong in the Lord is all about developing character and being mature.

Amplified Version says, "...be strong in the Lord [draw your strength from Him and be empowered through your union with Him] and in the power of His [boundless] might." This scripture gives us a clear focus – we are encouraged to **"... be strong in the Lord."**

The direction we look in during our struggles is to the Lord our God.
We draw our strength for this battle from our relationship with God because we know we are united with Him in salvation. To be empowered means we draw our strength from God knowing that His boundless power resides within us. What do we draw upon? The supernatural ability that was released when the Holy Spirit raised Jesus from death. It's all about our focus. In the day we fight we look to Jesus. The devil is defeated.

What do we draw upon? The power of the Holy Spirit within us. We draw upon the fire of the Spirit, the authority of the risen Christ, we draw upon the dominion of our God who wrested victory from Satan's grasp and gave it to us in Jesus name! We know that Satan and all of his cohorts were defeated by the resurrection of Jesus Christ and that Jesus gave us this victory as well!

We stir our faith in the word of the sovereign God and stand in the strength of His power. We move into the challenge, knowing that to stand strong we must look to God. The Lord is our champion. There is a joining together of the Holy Spirit's power in us and our knowledge of God's word upon which we stand our ground. We stir up our minds by way of remembrance – knowing what God's word says, not just reading it but remembering it and using it. His word will be a light to our path, and His word is alive and has authority and power.

We face challenges knowing that the Lord is with us. We stand up to the challenge knowing that God will be strong on our behalf. We keep our focus on the power of God, not the force of the enemy. Paul instructs us to be strong, to know that God's Spirit is within us. Be strong knowing that the word of God is within us.

Psalms 121: 1 -2 says, "I lift up my eyes to the mountains – where does my help come from? My help comes from the Lord, the Maker of heaven and earth."

The reason we look to the Lord is our help comes from Him. Our victory has been bought by Him. We look to the Lord because He remains our focus, He has our attention. Our efforts are not to focus on the enemy but to Him who has given us the victory over our enemy.

Listen to these remarkable words of Jesus in **Luke 10: 18 – 20 TPT** "I watched Satan topple until he fell suddenly from heaven like lightning to the ground. Now you understand that I have imparted to you all my authority to trample over his kingdom. You will trample upon every demon before you and overcome every power Satan possesses. Absolutely nothing will be able to harm you as you walk in this authority. However, your real source of joy isn't merely that these spirits submit to your authority, but that your names are written in the journals of heaven and that you belong to God's kingdom. This is the true source of your authority."

I love this! Jesus says He has imparted to us all of His authority to crush Satan's kingdom, including every demon. We will walk in safety, and **no harm** will come to us as we keep our eyes on Jesus and what He has done for us. The real source of our authority is found in Jesus name and the fact we are named as part of His kingdom and rule.

Our responsibility is to be clothed in the armour of God to withstand the onslaught of the enemy.
Paul says it twice – so it's doubly important. "Put on the full armour of God." The emphasis of the original language is that we "sink into these garments." The application is to "walk continually wearing this armour." There is never a time we should NOT be clothed with these things. We put on this supernatural armour knowing this amazing fact – it is only as we cloth ourselves with this armour that we will be able to take our stand against our enemy successfully. Armour protects us. And our weapons are divinely empowered for our success.

2 Corinthians 10: 4 says, "The weapons we fight with are not the weapons of the world. On the contrary, they have divine power to demolish strongholds."

1 Corinthians 15: 57 – 58 says, "But thanks be to God! He gives us the victory through our Lord Jesus Christ. Therefore, my dear brothers and sisters, stand firm. Let nothing move you."

Standing firm in the finished work of Jesus Christ who died and rose again. Standing firm on the fact the grave is empty, and Jesus was raised to new life and gives us this new life. This is the foundation from where we are wrestling. This is the foundation of our belief as we stand our ground. This is our armour as we move forward against the gates of Hell as we build together His church.

Our enemy is spiritual in nature.
Paul goes on to describe the nature and essence of our wrestle as being "against the rulers, against the authorities, against the powers of this dark world and against the spiritual forces of evil in the heavenly realms." We struggle against spiritual powers. Our enemy comes against us with satanic schemes and strategies. Don't be fooled, it may look like flesh and blood, but the origin of our battle is spiritual and must be met with spiritual weapons.

Don't be overwhelmed by this fact, but we have an enemy with powerful resources. The scriptures say that, during the battle in Heaven, God threw Lucifer and a third of the angels out of Heaven and they became Satan and his demons. They are called "rulers, authorities, powers of darkness and spiritual forces of evil." These forces of evil are divine creations of God who have gone bad. They remain potent forces with nefarious schemes and strategies all ranged against us as God's creation.

There is a fascinating story found in the book of Daniel chapter 10. You can read it for yourself. It's a long passage and is worth the time to read it. In the biblical account, Daniel spent 21 days in prayer and fasting. The scripture tells of an angel who came to give Daniel understanding of a vision. I find it a compelling account of both angelic powers and the fight they wage on our behalf against rulers and spiritual forces of evil.

Daniel had set his face to seek the Lord because he had had a vision he could not explain. So he prayed. After 21 days an angel came to him. It was an incredible vision which left Daniel on his face, trembling and with no strength. The angel told him that he had been dispatched from God the moment he turned his face to seek the Lord. But he had been hindered in getting to Daniel. The hindrance lasted for 21 days!

The angel explains his journey and why he was hindered. **Daniel 10:13 says,** "... the prince of the Persian kingdom resisted me twenty-one days. Then Michael, one of the chief Princes, came to help me because I was detained there with the King of Persia."

This passage needs to be explained. The angel could not have been detained by a human king or prince. The context of the scripture seems to indicate the angel was being hindered by a demonic prince or power of the air. The angel referred to him as the Prince of Persia. An evil ruler of the unseen world who had responsibilities for the nation of Persia. This is an interesting and indeed remarkable biblical account. The angel dispatched from God withstood resistance for 21 days and couldn't break through without the assistance from Michael.

The angel said he was helped by Michael, one of the chief princes. The scripture refers to an archangel by this name. Jude 9 speaks of him by name! The angel sent to Daniel to help him had help in his battle against the Prince of Persia.

The passage in Daniel goes on to say that on his return journey the angel "... will return to fight against the prince of Persia, and when I go, the prince of Greece will come." Another evil emissary from Satan was to resist the angel on his return journey this one is called The Prince of Greece.

I find this chapter of Daniel downright fascinating. I find it profound. I find it illuminating to the unseen world of both angels and demons. According to the passage in Ephesians 6, these demonic forces are not flesh and blood but are the rulers, the authorities, the powers of this dark world and the spiritual forces of evil in the heavenly realms. These demonic forces have schemes, stratagems, tricks, plots, tactics and all sorts of manoeuvres, all of them aimed against us.

These demons have had millennia to perfect their ploys and plans. These spiritual forces of evil are experts in human language and psychology. They know our weakness, they watch humanity to find our frailty and vulnerability. These spirits are experts at human nature, human responses and human motivations. These spirits, though unseen, can see us and observe us. They observe our micro expressions, they observe our internal reactions as they play across our faces, our body language and in our voice. Interestingly, they are like psychologists and psychiatrists, only they don't want us to get better. They do not have our best interests at heart. They want to destroy us.

Their agenda is nefarious! This is a reason why in the late 1800s and early 1900s the role of a psychiatrist or "alienist" was regarded by many as demonic or occultic and not real medicine. How could this "science of the mind" be trusted to be hard evidence and not the machinations of evil powers?

Note These demon spirits are revengeful. They hate God and desire to destroy the image of God found in humanity. Jesus put it this way in **John 10:10**, "The thief comes to steal kill and destroy." Thankfully Jesus comes to give us life and life more abundantly.

The New Testament teaches us that Satan appears as an angel of light. **2 Corinthians 11:14** says, "Satan himself masquerades as an angel of light." Masquerades – disguises himself – it's his cover-up – he pretends to be the truth but is in fact deceit. He comes to us pretending to be light – pretending to be the truth.

What Satan seeks to communicate to us is so close to the truth – so much so we will have a hard time telling his lies from God's truth. The devil seeks to bring people into our lives to offer us things that are so similar and so close to what God says. The devil will give you opportunities so close to what God has for you, but the end of it will be death. Unless you have an authenticating light or an objective standard that you can use to verify with you will never be able to tell with your physical eyes or ears whether this is the truth. We need the word of God and the illuminating work of the Holy Spirit.

Charles Spurgeon an English preacher from the mid-1800s once said, "Discernment is not knowing the difference between right and wrong. It is knowing the difference between right and almost right."

1 Corinthians 12: 10 again gives us insights into one of the gifts of the Spirit ... "to another distinguishing between spirits." Note the discernment is between spirits. This gift gives discernment as to whether an action is motivated by good or evil. The devil's forte, his big plan, is to deceive us. He works with deceit, it is his stock in trade – he is treacherous – he is the "father of lies" according to Jesus. This gift of the Spirit helps us to identify between the demonic, the human and the actions of God.

John 8:44 says, "The devil, was a murderer from the beginning, not holding to the truth, for there is no truth in him. When he lies, he speaks his native language, for he is a liar and the father of lies." We need more than human wisdom to defeat this kind of enemy. We need more than human discernment to overcome this kind of adversary. We need a light to help us to see and know the truth. We need the work of God's Spirit and God's word.

Challenge will come.
Paul says, *"...when the day of evil comes"* not if a day of evil comes. This is my crucial comment today – in the day of the challenge will you be up for it? The day will come. Throughout our lives, we will face these days of challenge regularly. Will you be up for the challenge?

In a lot of contemporary preaching and teaching these days it seems like there is an emphasis on tough times and going through tough times. This is good. People need to understand the principles of God's word as it applies to our contemporary problems. There's a lot of teaching that gives us encouragement to keep on going when tough time comes. Jesus was pretty clear when He said in **John 16: 33** "In this world, you will have trouble. But take heart! I have overcome the world."

The "day of evil" is that day when we will struggle and wrestle with tribulation, trouble and people who seek us harm. Paul speaks of it poetically as the "day of evil", and he instructs us that on that day we will stand strong, wearing a supernatural armour that will protect us and give us victory in the fight.

This is how we will face that evil day.
On that day of evil we are told twice to "put on the full armour of God." The same Greek word is found in **Ephesians 4:24** when we are encouraged "to put on the new self" and be like God in righteousness. The instruction to "put on" does not suggest that we would ever "take it off" but instead the instruction is to walk in it and live in it. Our armour is part of who we become as we walk with Jesus Christ. It's not something we take off at the end of every night. God's armour is intrinsic to who we are.

The scripture encourages us to stand our ground in the midst of the battle, in the evil day. We stand our ground having clothed ourselves with armour that will become who we are in Jesus.

Chapter 3
The belt of truth

"There is here a cruel dilemma before us. If we promoted justice and charity among men, we should be playing directly into the Enemy's hands; but if we guide them to the opposite behaviour, this sooner or later produces (for He permits it to produce) a war or a revolution, and the undisguisable issue of cowardice or courage awakes thousands of men from moral stupor. This, indeed, is probably one of the Enemy's motives for creating a dangerous world—a world in which moral issues really come to the point."
C.S. Lewis, "The Screwtape Letters"

"Demons don't play by the rules. They lie, and they cheat, and they stab you in the back."
Alan Grant,
Fictional character from Jurassic Park

"You are the offspring of your father, the devil, and you serve your father very well, passionately carrying out his desires. He's been a murderer right from the start! He never stood with the One who is the true Prince, for he's full of nothing but lies—lying is his native tongue. He is a master of deception and the father of lies!"
John 8:44

In **Acts 16: 17** Paul and his company met a woman possessed by a demon that was able to tell fortunes and use clairvoyance. She cried out when she saw Paul and said, "These men are servants of the Most High God who are telling you the way to be saved."

Now not everyone who tells fortunes or acts as a clairvoyant have demons, some are just charlatans. But there are some who are possessed by a spirit of clairvoyance and are under the direct control and manipulation of demons. This woman was one of those people. She had a demon residing inside of her.

What she was shouting out was true and correct, but after a few days of this, the scripture says Paul became so annoyed that he turned and said to the spirit "In the name of Jesus come out of her!"

What the demon was saying was right – Paul and his company were from God and were preaching a message of truth that would lead to salvation. However, the demon's word through the woman had become an annoying distraction to Paul's preaching. Her comments were the comments of a demon and they lacked integrity. It was a demon shouting it out, and Paul saw right through what was being done. Paul discerned the origins of the comment and realised it was a demon speaking, seeking to interrupt and distract from Paul's preaching and Paul dealt with the demon by casting it out of this woman.

There is a difference between truth and almost truth. This is a great strategy of the Devil; to speak "almost" truth. Integrity deals with reality. "**Integrity**" The word means sound, whole and intact. If something has integrity it means it will hold together firmly, it won't fall apart, even under pressure. Integrity is the state of being whole and undivided. Integrity is being sound or intact or healthy. It speaks of being blameless, innocent and operational. Integrity speaks of truth.

Ephesians 6: 13 – 14 says, "Therefore put on the full armour of God, so that when the day of evil comes, you may be able to stand your ground, and after you have done everything, to stand. Stand firm then, **with the belt of truth buckled around your waist**."

Let me tell you about the belt of truth.
I'm sure Paul would have waxed eloquent with this sermon. Using the belt to describe integrity and truth. A belt was the first piece of equipment put on when a Roman soldier went into war. The belt secures all the other sections of the armour. The belt of truth is integral to the full armour as it brings a sense of wholeness or soundness to the rest of the armour. The belt connects everything together. Wearing the belt showed that the soldier was ready for action since he would only loosen his belt when he went off duty or the battle was won!

In **Revelation 1: 13** Jesus is said to be standing before John with His girdle or belt over his shoulder – this shows Jesus at rest, the battle won, the battle finished, the victory delivered and Jesus once and forever the triumphant One who reigns supreme in and over all battles. We need to remember this.

In Roman times, the belt about the waist held together the soldier's garments, which might otherwise hamper his movements while marching or engaging in combat. The belt secured all the other pieces of the armour in their place. It was essential to have the belt fitted correctly as it brought integrity to the whole armour.

The spiritual significance is that God does not merely want us to point at the truth or even speak the truth; more than anything He wants us to BE TRUTH, to wear truth and have truth wrapped about us. Truth in our innermost being. To be bearers of truth – to walk in truth – to be the truth – this is the source of our personal integrity and is a powerful piece of our armour as we resist the devil in the day of evil! The greatest counter to the Devils lies is the truth, God's truth. We win the battle with truth and deep integrity.

2 Corinthians 3: 2 – 3 says, "You yourselves are ***our letter, written on our hearts, known and read by everyone. You show that you are a letter from Christ,*** the result of our ministry, written not with ink but with the Spirit of the living God, not on tablets of stone but on tablets of human hearts."

We are letters. We are the only Bible others may ever see. We walk in the truth of God's word, living out the truth of scripture. We are known, and we are read by everyone! People read us – they read our behaviour, our actions, our words and our lives. If there were no Bible others could read, they should be able to read us as we are letters written from Christ to a world in need of grace and truth.

The Belt of Truth is our integrity – based, founded and formed in the crucible of God's word. It is written in our hearts by the Holy Spirit. God's word is truth, and it is inscribed upon our hearts, and it forms the very foundation of our lives. God's truth living in us is the foundation of our integrity. We become operational only when the integrity quota is high in our personal lives.

When we wear it, we become it. It takes a tough and deliberate decision to disobey God's word knowingly; usually, our integrity will inform us, and we will live accordingly. This is integrity. Integrity is us living out Gods Truth – walking on the word of God. His word becomes an everlasting lamp unto our feet. We know the word of God, it becomes the compass of our heart, and it directs our every decision. When we walk in integrity, we are using the belt of truth to defeat the enemy's actions towards us.

Integrity is a vital piece of the equipment that gives our life meaning, direction and ultimate success. Integrity is telling myself the truth and honesty telling the truth to other people. This holds our life together. Integrity's reward is mostly an internal phenomenon: self-respect, dignity and self-esteem. Not doing right may have momentary payoffs but will wreak havoc with your self-esteem, respect from others and your quality of life. Integrity, or lack thereof, is what characterises people. You can easily judge the character of a man by how he treats those who can do nothing for him.

Muhammad Ali, professional boxer, once said, "I don't trust anyone who's nice to me but rude to the waiter. Because they would treat me the same way if I were in that position." This is another definition of integrity.

Douglas MacArthur, an American 5 star general and Field Marshal of the Philippines Army, once said, "A true leader has the confidence to stand alone, the courage to make tough decisions, and the compassion to listen to the needs of others. He does not set out to be a leader, but becomes one by the equality of his actions and the integrity of his intent."

But integrity is so much more than a requirement for leadership – although in life we are all leaders somewhere. Integrity is a vital piece of equipment in life for us all. Integrity ensures we have inner peace and self-respect.

Integrity is fundamental to walking in truth. Integrity holds every other part of our lives together. Integrity is a requirement in love – for marriage – in a family – between siblings and between friends. Integrity is a requirement in business – honesty between co-workers – truth between the employer and the employee. Integrity should be a prerequisite for all politicians; unfortunately we don't see much of this in their baffling actions on the world stage. Integrity is the basis upon how we treat other people and act in the world around us.

Integrity is more than reputation – **Abraham Lincoln** former President of the United States once said, *"Character is like a tree and reputation like a shadow. The shadow is what we think of it; the tree is the real thing."*

Proverbs 10:9 (NIVUK) says "Whoever walks in integrity walks securely, but whoever takes crooked paths will be found out." Integrity is a crucial element for success in every part of our life and existence – walking with nothing to hide – as those on the crooked path will be found out – exposed. Their duplicity will be revealed. This is embarrassing and causes people to stumble in the evil day.

Proverbs 11:3 (NIVUK) says, "The integrity of the upright guides them, but the unfaithful are destroyed by their duplicity." Integrity informs our decisions on life and living. Integrity guides us and directs us in the way that is right. Paul says that when the evil day comes, we'll need the belt of truth if we are to succeed and experience victory in our struggles. With truth and integrity as the foundations of our lives, we can fight any and every battle and win outright because we are walking in truth with the integrity of heart. Like a Roman soldier, we will need our belt. The thing that holds everything else in place. Without this, we are not going to be ready on the day of battle.

3 John 4 says "I have no greater joy than to hear that my children are walking in the truth." No greater joy!

Our enemy is the devil – Paul stresses we don't struggle against flesh and blood but against the spiritual forces of evil. Your struggle may look remarkably like "flesh and blood", but it really is a spiritual battle. Integrity is an ingredient of our spirit and keeps us living in victory. Truth triumphs always.

The battle plan the enemy has mapped out is for you to lose your integrity and to walk in something other than the truth. The enemy wants to compromise you. Not just in one action but to compromise the fundamentals of your life. The enemy wants to compromise your character to the extent it becomes a habit of your life.

Proverbs 25:26 says, (TPT) "When a lover of God gives in and compromises with wickedness, it can be compared to contaminating a stream with sewage or polluting a fountain." You can't win against the Devil if you're living in compromise.

The Devil will use people to attack you to incite actions that lack integrity but never forget the battle is spiritual. We'll still need wisdom to interact with people, but the source of the battle is spiritual.

As a developer of leaders, I have watched as extraordinarily gifted and talented people have fallen from prominence or been hindered in their rise to prominence because of fatal flaws of character repeated over and over again. Somewhere in their youth, they allowed the enemy to compromise their character to the extent it became a habit of hiding the truth to stay "OK" with others. But discerning leaders see the compromise.

As leaders, we identify the fatal flaw and seek to bring correction. We will seek to redeem them through godly discipline. In the lives of the sincere, we find we succeed, and they heed the correction and come back onto course. But in the lives of those who are not willing to pay the price of discipline they will continue to struggle. For whatever reason, they are not willing and refuse to move on to a life of transparent integrity and in their struggle against the forces of evil they find themselves compromised. As Paul says in **Ephesians 4:27** they give the enemy a "foothold" which is a wedge the enemy uses to keep us from success.

John Wooden, head coach for UCLA basketball team once said, "While you, the leader, can teach many things, character is not taught easily to adults who arrive at your desk lacking it. Be cautious about taking on reclamation projects regardless of the talent they may possess. Have the courage to make character count among the qualities you seek in others."

Our struggle is against spiritual powers. The enemy comes with satanic schemes and strategies designed to compromise our integrity. Plots and ploys. These ploys are designed by Satan to destroy the image of God within us. These plots are designed to trip us up and make us less effective as we walk with God. These plots are often launched by flesh and blood people, but their design is forged in Hell. It may be immorality or repeated unethical behaviour. It may be lying or having a disdain of truth. It may be anger or an inability to handle money. It may be a constant desire to sabotage others by sowing doubt or criticising someone. All of these things are designed in Hell to destroy you and compromise you.

Integrity is the true essence of spiritual warfare. In the midst of a trial or struggle we merely stand in our integrity. It's not about yelling and shouting, rebuking and commanding it to be bound in Jesus' name! The true essence of spiritual warfare is found in deep repentance which creates integrity and sincere soul surgery which is the building block of character performed under the guidance of the Holy Spirit. Spiritual warfare is standing quietly in godly integrity refusing to be compromised when the opposite is being offered. Standing in the evil day with a belt of truth buckled up and ready for anything.

Integrity wins the day when we stand our ground in the day of evil. King David cried out to God, "... search me and see if there be any wicked way in me" (Psalm 139.34 KJV). This is where we win the battle. Integrity or truth in our inner being keeps us on the road to victory and success.

We wrestle with our thoughts and our intentions – but integrity wins. We wrestle with what is right over what may just appear right – but integrity wins. We wrestle with our motivations – but integrity wins. We wrestle with our desires – but integrity wins. We wrestle with what's appropriate and what's not – but integrity wins. We wrestle with our language making sure it is appropriate and clean – but integrity wins. We wrestle with our interactions with people not allowing it to turn into sexually inappropriate actions – but integrity wins. We wrestle with temptation – but integrity wins.

It's our weapon of integrity that informs our walk with God.

Our most potent weapon against the enemy is truth internalised – God's word in the depths of our heart. We need more than human wisdom to defeat this kind of enemy. We need more than human discernment to overcome this kind of adversary. We need a light to help us to see and know the truth.

Galatians 5: 16 says, "But I say, walk by the Spirit, and you will not carry out the desire of the flesh." The word "walk" has as its meaning – "be occupied by" The emphasis is to "keep in step" with the Holy Spirit. Be guided by His promptings. Listen carefully to the voice of the Spirit.

Colossians 3:16 (TPT) says, "Let the word of Christ live in you richly, flooding you with all wisdom. Apply the Scriptures as you teach and instruct one another with the Psalms, and with festive praises, and with prophetic songs given to you spontaneously by the Spirit, so sing to God with all your hearts!"

In a world where truth is relative, we need an authenticating light and objective standard to guide our lives and be an eternal light to show the path. Jesus is that truth. He is the light that pierces that darkness. He is the light that reveals our paths. He is truth. To stand in the evil day, we will need to find ourselves with the courage of our convictions standing in truth and standing in our integrity.

Only by standing in God's word will we ever be able to stand in the day of evil against us. Our victory is in doing the right thing, combined with wisdom from God's word. Our victory is standing tall for what God says in His word.

Chapter 4
The breastplate of righteousness

"He cannot 'tempt' to virtue as we do to vice. He wants them to learn to walk and must, therefore, take away His hand; and if only the will to walk is really there, He is pleased even with their stumbles."
C.S. Lewis, "The Screwtape Letters"

"Not necessity, not desire - no, the love of power is the demon of men. Let them have everything - health, food, a place to live, entertainment - they are and remain unhappy and low-spirited: for the demon waits and waits and will be satisfied."
Friedrich Nietzsche

"This righteousness is given through faith in Jesus Christ to all who believe."
Romans 3:22

In my walk with God over 45 years, I have been the target of others who have sought to sully my name and reputation and discredit me in ways that could only be described as "satanic." I've been lied about, and rumours have circulated about me. Even well-meaning people have said hurtful and untrue things about me. Some people have a picture of me that may have been true about 30 years ago or 20 years ago but is no longer true about me now because I have grown and changed considerably.

I'd be lying if I said it didn't hurt. It does hurt – big time. But I learned a long time ago it's not what others call me- it's what I answer to!

Challenge will come! The evil day will come! Troubles, trials and tribulation are part of our human struggle. Lies, false witnesses will rise, and enemies will seek to destroy you out of their jealousy and insecurity. Doubt, disillusionment and disappoints will come. Social media will target you – websites will spring up dedicated to hating you! An email will be received, and it will seem outrageous the things they say about you. You'll hear the rumour and wonder what to do. But as God's people we put on God's armour and continue to walk forward with our heads held high. We know that discouragement is real! Sometimes it feels like a fight. And it is. Try "hand to hand" combat!

People! It appears that many of our troubling times and experiences are directly related to people. People criticise us, lie about us, betray us, get angry at us, and cause problems for us by just being human! Just interacting with people can be prickly and in some cases downright terrible. It's tough, and we wrestle with these situations and often times misidentify the real source of our conflict. Now don't get me wrong people are part of the equation, and we will need wisdom, grace and patience in dealing with people, but people are not the source of our conflicts.

We think its "flesh and blood" – I mean, it's got to be "flesh and blood" because it looks so much like "flesh and blood", but it isn't. I know what you're thinking right now: 'But Tom, it is people!' Yes! But the scripture shows us another truth. It may look and feel human, but it was forged in Hell. It is the truth, we wrestle with an unseen enemy, and we wrestle "against the authorities, against the powers of this dark world and against the spiritual forces of evil in the heavenly realms." The true nature of our struggles is spiritual, not natural. The source of our conflict is a spiritual dilemma, not an earthly predicament. A natural response would not defeat our spiritual enemy. The source of our troubles is not "THAT PERSON" but a spiritual power unseen by your natural eyes.

There is a spiritual realm. It is unseen by our human eyes. I find it interesting that as western Christians that we have to explain this truth, yet in other countries in Africa and Asia these truths are self-evident. In many of these countries and cultures, they believe in an unseen realm that has influence and interacts with their everyday life, and they know it's very real!

Christians often say: 'We mustn't see demons everywhere.' I do agree but *do we see them anywhere?!* Challenging hey?

Are we teaching the next generation about the truths and realities of this unseen realm? Are we teaching this next generation about the power of evil spirits, that they are real and very potent? Are we teaching them to be aware of the influence of these spiritual forces of evil? Do we understand the biblical mandate and instructions for dealing with them? Or do we use psychology 101 in dealing with criticism? Neuro-Linguistic Programming (NLP) for handling angry mobs? Nothing wrong with psychology or NLP but I think there is a deeper more evident truth in scripture. Paul says it, "Our struggle is not against flesh and blood" - no matter how much flesh and blood looks like it is the source!

Ephesians 6 is a rare glimpse in scripture to this unseen realm and gives pertinent and powerful instructions for dealing with the fight. I find it extraordinary that the scriptures would provide us with this kind of teaching about the unseen realm of demons and evil spirits.

Breastplate of Righteousness.
In the last chapter I wrote about the belt of truth – the part of God's armour that is integral to every other part. It is the truth that holds every other piece of the armour together and allows us to stand our ground in the fight.

Let me introduce you to the breastplate of righteousness. The breastplate of righteousness guards our heart. In battle, a wound to the chest can be fatal. That's why ancient soldiers wore a breastplate covering their heart and lungs. They knew they could be taken out if their hearts were pierced by the enemy's arrow or sword.

Your heart! The scriptures are full of instructions and encouragements to watch over it and protect it. Your heart is the seat of your affection, it's where you feel things. It is a place where we can feel the deepest hurt or the most sublime sense of dignity. You can have a broken heart[6], a hard heart[7], a heart that is blinded by darkness[8], a stony heart[9], a deceitful heart[10] or a pure heart[11].

Your heart is the thing which allows you to trust God and trust others and it is easily broken unless it is protected. It's with your heart you love. It's with your heart that you love God, worship God and love others. You give your heart or withhold it. In marriage, you give your heart to another, and they hold it. Scripture is clear you can give your whole heart, or you can hold back on giving your heart.

As in the natural, so in the spiritual, your heart is key to life. If your heart stops beating you will die. So in the spiritual, if you have a hardened heart, you will die spiritually. If you withhold love from your spouse, your marriage will be in peril. So it is if your heart becomes lukewarm towards Jesus, you lose your first love for Jesus and your spiritual life will suffer, and the enemy will have an advantage over you.

Proverbs 4:23 says, "Above all else, guard your heart, for everything you do flows from it."

From God's perspective, it is essential to protect our heart and so the breastplate. We're called to put on a breastplate of righteousness. So what is it about righteousness that protects us from the schemes of the spiritual forces of evil? Let's be clear here – the enemies plan is to destroy the image of God within us. To do that he employs many schemes. He has a multitude of plans and ploys, methods and designs to do damage to our heart

---

[6] Psalms 34:18

[7] Hebrews 3:8

[8] Ephesians 4:18

[9] Ezekiel 36:26

[10] Jeremiah 17:9

[11] Psalms 51:10

One of his plans is to accuse you. His name is found in **Revelation 12: 10** and it is "Accuser of the Brethren." The scripture says he accuses us before God "day and night." With our enemy, the Devil, there seems to be no holding back in his constant assault upon us.

His work against us is to sow doubt. He seeks to fill our lives with insecurity, fear and anxiety. The enemy works to cause us to feel distressed, to worry, to panic and to get stressed out over things. The enemy will lie to us. He will seek to deceive us, mislead us, con us, misinform us, cheat us, defraud us and dupe us into believing his lies. The enemy will bring people into our lives to hurt us, criticise us, malign us, and spread rumours about us and straight out lie about us. We want to respond to the flesh and blood attacks, but we need to react in a different spirit to the troubles that come our way!

The only way we can protect our hearts is to have it covered by the righteousness of God. This breastplate tells us we are not what the devils say we are. This righteousness of God tells us who we are in Jesus Christ and He reminds us to live the Spirit-filled life, to live obedient to God's word and to keep in step with the Holy Spirit. His righteousness implores us to live humbly in His presence.

Remember the scripture says "put on the full armour", every bit of it. When we compromise our integrity, it will be difficult to find the faith to believe that we are the righteousness of God in Christ. I said it would be a challenge, but we can still do it. But how much more convincing to our inner being if we are girt with a belt of integrity as well as righteousness.

The breastplate protects our hearts, encouraging us not just to receive Christ's righteousness imputed through salvation but to walk in God's righteousness! The righteousness of Christ is a powerful concept in New Testament theology. It informs us as to who we are, who we belong to and where we stand. The righteousness of Christ speaks powerfully to our standing in God's presence. Let me explain.

2 Corinthians 5:21 says, "God made him who had no sin to be sin for us so that in him we might become the righteousness of God."
Romans 5: 1 – 5 says, "Therefore, since we have been justified through faith, we have peace with God through our Lord Jesus Christ, through whom we have gained access by faith into this grace in which we now

stand. And we boast in the hope of the glory of God. Not only so, but we also glory in our sufferings, because we know that suffering produces perseverance; perseverance, character; and character, hope. And hope does not put us to shame, because God's love has been poured out into our hearts through the Holy Spirit, who has been given to us."

Because of Jesus, His substitutionary death, His powerful resurrection and His glorious ascent back to Heaven at God's right hand we have now, by our faith in Jesus, been justified – just as if we had never sinned against God or Heaven. This justification means we are without sin and hence no guilt, no condemnation and no shame – we have been forgiven, and this is by faith – not by works. Imputed to each Christian is the righteousness of Christ. The Bible declares we are the righteousness of God in Christ! It matters very little what the Devil says to us. We know we have peace with God.

When the enemy of our heart and soul attacks us, we respond by being clothed with the fabric of who we are in Christ. The armour is impenetrable to guilt, shame, condemnation and anxious thoughts. Our hearts are protected by His righteousness. We are not who the enemy says we are. We have a new standing.

This new standing has given us peace with God. There is no anger, no strife and no malice between God and me. There is no judgement or condemnation either. This standing we have comes through Jesus Christ because of His death and resurrection. No matter how I feel or think or experience the world around me, no matter what my enemy says about me, I am the righteousness of God in Christ. God is no longer angry with me but has shown His great love and acceptance of me. ***This is what is called GRACE!*** It is in this grace we stand, not fall, but stand! Even in the evil day, we stand and do not fall. The enemy's action towards us fails when we know who we are in Christ.

Because of Jesus, we have gained access by faith into His grace. His grace is this undeserved advantage we possess. This grace gives us standing in His presence where we have no sin, no shame, no guilt and our conscience is clear. We have a righteousness that has been imputed, credited to our account or given to us as an act of grace through faith that provides us with unfettered access to God's presence. We stand covered by His righteousness. This is our victory when the enemy comes to judge us or condemn us. Our hearts are protected from his damaging work, and we stand in the righteousness of Christ.

Hebrews 4:16 declares, "Let us then approach God's throne of grace with confidence, so that we may receive mercy and find grace to help us in our time of need."

We approach boldly, with confidence that we are acceptable in His sight. There is no fear, no shame and no condemnation. At this moment we find grace in our time of need. Our struggle is then not for victory but from victory. We declare we are the righteousness of Christ and as we walk in that truth we defeat the enemy in his attack upon us.

- The breastplate that protects our heart and spirit is His righteousness.
- With this righteousness imputed to us, we are able to stand up to every accusation the devil makes about us.
- We can come confidently to God because we are the righteousness of God in Christ
- Peace becomes the state of faith we stand in.
- Grace is what we walk in. His grace is so sufficient even when we feel weak!
- Righteousness is what makes it possible to stand in God presence without feeling inferior guilty or ashamed. It is the righteousness of God in Christ. We got here because of His salvation so rich and expansive.

When the devil comes and seeks to attack our hearts, we have the truth of God's righteousness that protects us. When the enemy comes against us with the unexpected and with what seems like overwhelming numbers, we stand. Maybe shaken but not counted out! Maybe knocked down but not knocked out! Even the deadliest blow of the enemy is deflected by the breastplate of righteousness. In the day of struggle, we stand on the battleground and declare we are the righteousness of God in Christ. When we do, we win.

It guards the front.
Notice it is a breastplate – it guards the front of us – there is no protective covering for our back – this is because when we stand our ground, we always have someone else to guard our back. Many Roman soldiers would fight back to back guarding each other's back as they fight their enemy. We have others to guard our backs too – they are members of the church – there will be someone to have your back.

Some smirk here because of bad experiences in church. But stop. If you are in right relationship with God, more than likely, you'll be in right relationship with God's church too. The opposite is also true. You being in right relationship with the local church is paramount in importance, especially when you are in a battle for your very soul.

People say to me, "I can be a Christian and not go to church." I say, "True but for how long can you maintain that?" The writer to the **Hebrews 10:25** was correct that we should "not give up meeting together." The writer actually says to "encourage one another" to make every effort to be part of the gathering. Never underestimate the power of the "Gathering!" Be a part of a local church. Don't get into the habit of missing the gathering, it will not help you in your struggles against the forces of evil.

And no, it's not a dream, the church is far from perfect, but it is where God says He will provide back up in the day of trouble. If we are to receive back up, we must learn to trust leadership and guard our heart against "taking" offence. Don't allow offence to make you disconnect from the life-giving energy of the church. Stay connected.

Should the horrible day of evil arrive, and you have no backup from God's people then according to **Isaiah 52: 12** "... the God of Israel will be your rear guard!" He will remain our faithful Shepherd. My strong advice is to find yourself in a church where you will be under the oversight of godly leaders who have your best interests at heart and will protect your back in the day of trouble. There is no perfect church – just like there are no perfect Christians. Get over offence quickly.

How do we put on this breastplate? Certainly, this is by an act of faith in God's word. Jesus said, "It is finished." But God's commandments are righteousness, and we can put on this breastplate by faith and by simply walking in and obeying God in our lives. You don't do this over a morning devotional. It's a lifestyle of simply living the word of God on a daily basis. I find this is a problem with God's people. They are disobedient because they are mostly ignorant of God's principles of living. They don't read God's word, they don't study, and if they do, they chose not to follow what the word of God says. They wonder why they are so exposed in this spiritual warfare. Hide God's word in your heart, and you will find it will protect you in the day of evil.

Chapter 5
Feet fitted with the readiness of the Gospel

"We want a whole race perpetually in pursuit of the rainbow's end, never honest, nor kind, nor happy now, but always using as mere fuel wherewith to heap the altar of the future every real gift which is offered them in the Present."
C.S. Lewis, "The Screwtape Letters"

"Demons do not exist anymore than gods do, being only the products of the psychic activity of man."
Sigmund Freud

"Never be lacking in zeal, but keep your spiritual fervour, serving the Lord."
Romans 12:11

As a missionary in Thailand, I had numerous confrontations with people under the control of an evil spirit. On one instance I was ministering with another Australian pastor in the city of Pattaya. During my friend's message, a young 19-year-old Thai woman stood to her feet. I saw her from my peripheral vision but thought little of it as – you know – people get up and move around a lot during services!

But this was different. As she stood, she went rigid and began to shake. Within a few seconds, she started to cry out with a blood-curdling scream! Obviously, people were shaken. A group of Thai men went towards her and wanted to help her to her seat, but she fought them off! It was amazing to watch. She was all of 55 kilos (120 lbs) and of small stature. I looked to my Aussie pastor mate wondering what he would do as he did have the platform. I saw his face drain of blood as he stood stock-still wondering what was happening! To be honest, it was a loud scream, and the sound would send chills through almost anyone who was unprepared.

The 3 or 4 guys who stood up to help the woman to her seat were being thrown off her like rag dolls from a kids pram. I knew I needed to do something and swiftly. Amazingly 10 seconds had passed, and she was still screaming in a very frighteningly way! So, I got up and walked over towards her and said, "In the name of Jesus Christ be still and be silent!" I didn't yell or even raise my voice. But immediately the young woman stopped and quietly slumped to the ground. But her eyes were still open, and she did not look like she was happy. I, however, merely stood my ground. I knew what I was dealing with but did the evil spirit in her know what it was dealing with?

So I spoke again, "In the name of Jesus Christ I command you to come out of her!" It was obvious I was not speaking to the woman but the spirit inside her. The screaming had stopped, but the young woman began to convulse. Not a pretty sight. But I insisted again in Jesus' name for the spirit to come out of her. In less than 30 seconds there was what appeared to be one last big convulsion, and she went silent, still laying on the floor of the church. In my spirit, I knew the evil spirit had left her. So did a few others in the room as they began to praise God.

I calmed the young woman down a bit and realised I had amazingly conducted this exorcism in English because I now reverted to Thai as I spoke to her. As I tried to get her to her seat, I had a word of knowledge. The Holy Spirit revealed to me that there had been some kind of amulet given to her at one time and this amulet was now on her body and had acted as an open door or wedge, for the spirit to control her. I asked if this was true and she said it was. I asked to see the amulet. It was on her wrist. I asked where she got it from and she told me this story:

The year previous she had been very sick with a wasting disease that caused her to be sick, tired, and listless, to have no appetite and caused her insomnia. Her mother suggested she go to a Buddhist priest known for healing cures and she did. The priest gave her the amulet after offering "prayers" over it. She attached it to her wrist, and miraculously she began to recover very quickly. She also started having dreadful dreams at night that left her feeling distressed the next day. She was being terrorised by these dreams for nearly a year when she found her way into our church and into our meeting.

I asked her if she would be willing to give me the amulet. She immediately removed it from her wrist. As a church, we prayed for her then and there for God to bring healing in Jesus' name! Obviously, I destroyed the amulet and of course stayed in touch with the church and it was reported she has been in good health since then, with no recurring dreams of terror. She had been set free from demon control and healed by the power of Jesus name! It was a great miracle. It was a great victory too for Jesus, overcoming evil in her life and bringing peace to her terrorised life. It remains a great story!

The Gospel of Peace.
Ephesians 6: 15 says, "Stand firm then, with the belt of truth buckled around your waist, with the breastplate of righteousness in place, and ***with your feet fitted with the readiness that comes from the gospel of peace.***

Spiritual warfare is real! But Paul gives us insights into how to prepare for the fight. It's not to be the aggressor either. It's not in our attack but in our readiness. We are to stand our ground and speak the powerful message of the Gospel. Remember, in our struggles, there's no place for a retreat! We're called to stand our ground and never back away; "...and after you have done everything, to stand. Stand firm then."

Abraham Lincoln once said, "Be sure you put your feet in the right place, then stand firm."

1 Corinthians 16: 13 says, "Be on your guard; stand firm in the faith; be courageous; be strong."

1 Corinthians 15: 58 says, "Therefore, my beloved brothers, be steadfast, immovable, always abounding in the work of the Lord, knowing that in the Lord your labour is not in vain."

I'm not talking about being obstinate, opinionated or just being stubborn. No, Paul speaks of our stand in truth and not retreating from what we know and believe. This is how we do spiritual warfare: we resist evil with the reality of the Gospel of Christ. The battle is won by our refusal to move backwards. The struggle may continue, but we stand and resist it daily!

In our ongoing struggle against the spiritual forces of evil, God has given us a clear picture of how to protect ourselves or to "take our stand against" those schemes of the devil. Paul instructs us to have our feet ***"fitted with the readiness that comes from the gospel of peace."*** Let's break this down, because it is a fascinating thing to consider in our wrestle against the "powers of this dark world."

The most obvious picture is that of a Roman soldier's sandals. They were made of leather, with three layers being used. They were open toed and with straps that were tied up the leg or around the ankles of the solider. On the soles, there were spikes to keep a grip on the terrain, used to fight against a fallen enemy, and they were tough for the long marches they were required to take.

So how does this apply to us as we take a stand against the enemy and his schemes?

This part of the armour speaks of **readiness** – it speaks of our eagerness, of our enthusiasm or passion. It speaks of our confidence and fearlessness. It speaks of our willingness to stand firm. It also speaks about our willingness to share the good news about Jesus with whoever we can. Being ready means we are equipped and prepared but with a keenness described as passion!

1 Peter 3: 15 says, "But in your hearts revere Christ as Lord. Always be prepared to give an answer to everyone who asks you to give the reason for the hope that you have. But do this with gentleness and respect."

The Message translation says it his way, "Be ready to speak up and tell anyone who asks why you're living the way you are, and always with the utmost courtesy." It's our readiness, our passion and our purpose of sharing the message of Christ that is crucial when we are called to stand "when the day of evil arrives." This is why I love the preaching of the gospel with passion because it is in our readiness to do so that defeats the enemy.

- Our passion is "our first love", which we are told not to forsake.
- With a white hot passion for Jesus, we will be able to stand in the day of evil.
- The fiery trial will seek to burn us up and burn us out, but passion will keep us burning with God's power. God's fire is no match for the fire of any trial.

How do we do the Christian life without passion? Scripture tells us it is possible, but it's not the preferred position. No, we must have our feet shod with the readiness of the gospel of peace! Feet ready to move with passion to defeat the enemy.

Romans 12:9 – 13, says "Love must be sincere. Hate what is evil; cling to what is right. Be devoted to one another in love. Honour one another above yourselves. ***Never be lacking in zeal, but keep your spiritual fervour, serving the Lord.*** Be joyful in hope, patient in affliction, and faithful in prayer. Share with the Lord's people who are in need. Practise hospitality."

Never lacking in zeal – so it must be possible to lack zeal. But Paul says we must never lack it. His encouragement is to keep our spiritual fervour, serving the Lord. It's awful when you lose your zeal – you merely become ineffectual. Zeal is for serving and when we lose our zeal we quit serving God and others. This then gives the enemy a foothold.

We are called upon to do these things with passion! Our readiness and passion will give us a sure footing in our struggles against spiritual forces of evil. The Devil finds it tough to distract us with his ploys and schemes when we're passionate about helping and serving people.

I love that these shoes were meant **for the long haul**. Too many have had a great start but a lousy finish. They seem to be on fire, full on and then they wane in their enthusiasm and wonder why the enemy seems to be pushing a wedge between them and God. They are "heart and soul... until!" Until they find a girlfriend or boyfriend; until they get engaged; until they get married or have children or until they find that dream job. Until something better comes along, until something more important to them takes their time and focus off God. Until the enemy can distract them with a whole host of good and bad things. Let's face it getting married isn't bad but it can distract from our love of God and severely hijack our Christian experience. God wants us to enjoy all the good things, marriage included, but not at the cost of our passion for Him.

There are loads of reason why people flag in their zeal. To the 30 somethings reading this – you may have felt like you were going to turn the world upside down by now and you've not reached all of your goals. To you I say – don't give up – you've only just started! You have a lifetime to achieve your goals and plenty of time to make a huge difference in the world around you still. Just a hint though, rather than making a goal for prominent success how about making a goal of long-term significance.

To the 60 somethings reading this you may have felt "What is going on with the church these days!" You may be living in the glory of a church that is no longer, longing for the experiences you had 20 or 30 years ago. Lamenting that the young leaders are not like the heroes of your faith. My advice is don't live in the past, but be excited about today!

The church has adapted to the times, same message but different packaging. Stop being critical of what the church has become. Learn to be aware of the times. I know you were hippies back in your day, but church life has changed significantly. Get with the times and stop whining about what the church used to be. God is still there! The music is different, and we use a projector on a screen instead of the chorus books and the red Redemption Hymnal but the Spirit is still moving, and thousands are being saved. Stop being so negative. Get back your passion and love these beautiful young people, you don't need a father in the faith anymore, become a father or mother in the faith. Remember, the best is yet to come! The enemy will compromise your passion by blunting it with societal changes and your response to them. Don't allow your enemy that pleasure. Defeat the enemy by being white hot in your passion for Jesus and His church. He is manifest even in a church with smoke machines, a darkened room and LCD screens!

Stay passionate.
In most cases, I see other more nefarious things at work to blunt our zeal and passion. In **Ephesians 4: 27** we are warned not to allow the devil a **foothold** in our lives. We're encouraged that as we deal with issues that it is ok to be angry, but not with a sense of revenge or of holding a grudge. Because if we do we will give the devil a foothold in our lives – it will be like a wedge driven between God and us. The enemy wins when we won't deal with crucial issues in our life. Whether its anger, unforgiveness or bitterness, we actually open up our lives to the enemy who gains a foothold over us if we refuse to deal with issues. Saying passionate is the key to winning in our struggles. Passion defeats the enemy every time!

We wonder about a breakthrough, we pray for victory and yet really it's all about us letting go of things and stop giving the enemy a foothold in our lives. We allow stress to rule us, we allow anxiety to dominate us, and we allow cynicism to be our perspective. To stand our ground and live as more than conquerors we need to make sure we remain passionate for God, His church and His gospel and remove these wedges that drive us from God. The older we get, the more stuff we'll need to deal with – stuff that could compromise our passion.

Paul heeds us, beseeches us in **2 Corinthians 2: 10 – 11,** speaking on the theme of forgiveness he says, "I have forgiven in the sight of Christ for your sake *so that Satan might not outwit us*. For we are not unaware of his schemes."

Paul makes a startling and stinging comment. Satan can outwit us! He can out think, out manoeuvre and out scheme us if we hang on to unforgiveness, bitterness, offence or any issues that get in our way of living a life devoted to God. Paul heeds us not to be ignorant of Satan's schemes.

The devil is not afraid of a Christian. The devil is afraid of a passionate Christian! When we lose our passion for God and His glorious message of salvation for the world we begin to make excuses for not sharing our faith with others. We're compromised. When we lose our passion, we find ourselves embarrassed about our relationship with Christ. It's when we lose our passion that we find ourselves conceding in the battle. It's when we are no longer fitted with a readiness to share the gospel of peace, when we grow weary of church and when we stop being amazed by God's word it's then we give the enemy a sure foothold in our lives. To see victory in our struggle we need to put on the shoes fitted with readiness.

If we are not diligent in keeping our passion alive for Jesus and our salvation we won't make it for the long haul. We'll settle for less. We'll settle for comfort and the status quo. We'll settle for a grudge or unforgiveness instead of growing up and moving on in our journey. We will settle for a personal faith rather than one you can share with others and bring them to church. We will settle for a sense of disappointment in the "way the church is going", proclaiming to be a Christian but in truth have stopped being involved in the gathering. I don't want to settle for anything less than God's best for my life.

1 Corinthians 9:24 – 27 says, "Do you not know that in a race all the runners run, but only one gets the prize? Run in such a way as to get the prize. Everyone who competes in the games goes into strict training. They do it to get a crown that will not last, but we do it to get a crown that will last forever. Therefore I do not run like someone running aimlessly; I do not fight like a boxer beating the air. No, I strike a blow to my body and make it my slave so that after I have preached to others, I myself will not be disqualified for the prize."

Paul uses the metaphor of a runner and a boxer. Runners run the race until they receive their prize. That means they have to finish the race. Everyone who competes goes into strict training – speaks of discipline. They do it to get a crown – a prize – a T-Shirt, a medal and a pint of cider – but that prize doesn't last.

Paul goes on to say that, as a Christian, we compete to get a crown that will last forever. Paul is speaking of our salvation, and it's all about our sense of purpose, our sense of destiny to make a difference in the world around us – it's all about leading people to a saving knowledge of Christ through the Gospel. It's about being part of a great church seeing people coming to Jesus on a regular basis. It's about being a mature believer helping to disciple others on the journey. It about being part of a praying, enthusiastic and passionate church where everything we do goes towards winning people to Jesus Christ. This attitude is a powerful attitude to possess.

Paul, changing the metaphor, goes on to say we don't fight like a boxer who merely beats the air. No, he says, I'm in this fight. I'm ready to knock a blow to the scheme of the enemy. I'll pray until something changes. I'll use my faith to move the mountain. I will stand my ground in the evil day and continue to stand. I will discipline my body, I will strike a blow to my body! I'll make it my slave! For this reason... so that after I have preached to others, I will not be disqualified for the prize – the eternal crown found in my relationship with Christ and realised when I arrive in Heaven.

This is a readiness to share the gospel of peace because *(and this is powerful – so don't miss this)* the gospel, as a message, has extraordinary, life-changing and explosive power in the spirit realm. Forces of evil are resisted, and the battle weathered as we speak this amazing message.

The message itself has power.
Romans 1: 16 says, "For I am not ashamed of the gospel, because it is the power of God that brings salvation to everyone who believes."

The greatest miracle in all the universe is for one person to come to faith in Jesus Christ. The greatest miracle is the salvation of one soul! No other miracles bring angels out to the ramparts of Heaven to rejoice and party like one sinner repenting. **Luke 15: 10** says, "In the same way, I tell you, there is rejoicing in the presence of the angels of God over one sinner who repents."

There is power released when we preach the gospel. There is a supernatural movement in the atmosphere when we share this message of all messages. There is an undefeatable church that grows when it commits to preaching the good news of Jesus. Christians remain victorious when their primary purpose in life is to share the powerful message of Jesus. Churches move forward as they preach the gospel, the power of God unto salvation. In these kinds of a church, not even the gates of Hell will prevail.

No wonder demons are repelled as we speak this message. It is a message of salvation for whoever believes, but it is a message that spells doom to the spiritual forces of evil. To the powers of darkness, this is a message of eternal damnation and punishment.

Preach this message – in season and out of season! In every one of our public services we preach the gospel and boldly give people an opportunity to respond by receiving Jesus as their saviour. The atmosphere turns electric as the preacher says, "I see that hand!" Spiritual power is being released in that moment. Life is being infused with resurrection power, the same spirit that raised Christ from the dead is quickening people as they pray! A life-altering alliance is being forged which does great damage to the kingdom of darkness. Not only is new life being released, forgiveness of sin and the removal of judgement, but there is a transference from being controlled by darkness to being controlled by light. The enemy loses again!

Colossians 1: 13 – 14 says it this way, "For he (Jesus) has rescued us from the dominion (control) of darkness and brought (transferred) us into the kingdom (authority) of the Son he loves, in whom we have redemption (being brought back), the forgiveness of sins." (Brackets added)

This is what takes place when the message is preached and people respond! They are rescued from Satan's power and authority over them. The preaching and declaring of this message sets the captive free. People are released from satanic bondage as we preach this message. Encapsulated in this message is the breaking of all satanic power ranged against us, curses are broken, generational torment is defeated, and people are set free. We are rescued by Jesus from Satan's dominion and his control over our lives. Jesus brings us into a new relationship with God, and we are brought into a kingdom where Jesus now reigns in authority over all darkness. We are redeemed, bought back from Satan's authority over our lives. The purchase price was the very blood of Jesus Christ as He was crucified for our sins. We find we have forgiveness, freedom and grace.

Ephesians 2: 1 – 5 says, "As for you, you were dead in your transgressions and sins, in which you used to live when you followed the ways of this world and of the ruler of the kingdom of the air, the spirit who is now at work in those who are disobedient. All of us also lived among them at one time, gratifying the cravings of our flesh and following its desires and thoughts. Like the rest, we were by nature deserving of wrath. But because of his great love for us, God, who is rich in mercy, made us alive with Christ even when we were dead in transgressions—it is by grace you have been saved."

God "makes us alive with Christ" and this resurrection power is great! More powerful than anything else in this world we live in! This power is released as we preach the message and as people respond! No demon in Hell can fight against this power. In salvation, we are no longer being controlled by "... the ruler of the kingdom of the air, the spirit who is now at work in those who are disobedient." Now we are controlled by the love of our Saviour Jesus Christ. Satan has no legal part of our lives.

We are, as Colossians says, "rescued!" The domination of the powers of darkness no longer have authority over us because we are redeemed – bought back from Satan – the purchase price was Jesus' death and resurrection! Demonic power is dethroned as one sinner repents and turns to Jesus.

People who respond to the message are then placed in a new alliance – into a new kingdom – into a new relationship. They are transferred into the Kingdom of Jesus Christ where He is Lord and God. This Jesus, who defeated death, Hell and sin, is now our new master and precious saviour! We no longer answer to the Devil's command but hear a new voice in our lives. The words of Jesus bring life and transformation on a daily level.

You see the very message of the Good News brings destruction to the Devil's kingdom. The very message is the power of God unto salvation, and this is the reason we must have our feet ***"fitted with the readiness that comes from the gospel of peace."***

This is why the church is so vital. This is why the church is so central to the message. This is why the church is so powerful. Jesus said He would build His church and in **Matthew 16:18** "the gates of Hades will not overcome it." Now gates don't move – so it must be the ongoing movement of the church taking ground from the enemy, and the enemy find themselves unable to stop this forward movement. This forward movement is when people wear those shoes of the gospel and never stop advancing! Passion will always win!

Chapter 6
The shield of faith

"He has filled His world full of pleasures. There are things for humans to do all day long without His minding in the least—sleeping, washing, eating, drinking, making love, playing, praying, and working. Everything has to be twisted before it's any use to us. We fight under cruel disadvantages. Nothing is naturally on our side."
C.S. Lewis, "The Screwtape Letters"

The most powerful weapon to conquer the devil is humility. For, as he does not know at all how to employ it, neither does he know how to defend himself from it.
St Vincent de Paul
A French Roman Catholic priest who dedicated himself to serving the poor.

"In him and through faith in him we may approach God with freedom and confidence."
Ephesians 3:12

I used to love it when visitors to Thailand would ask me about going into a Buddhist Temple. I mean, they are pretty. They help to describe Thai culture, and they help you to understand the religion of Thailand as well. So it was a teaching moment when we visited a temple.

Some, with fear in their voices, would ask me if I wasn't concerned I'd be jumped by evil spirits if I went into one. Why am I expected to take my shoes off at the threshold of the temple – isn't that honouring the spirits inside? Remember these were western Christians with little to no knowledge of Thai culture and religion – it was why they were here in the first place. So it was a teaching session.

In **Acts 19** there is a fascinating story about some Jewish exorcists, the seven sons of Sceva. **Verse 13** says they would speak to the evil spirits this way, "In the name of the Jesus whom Paul preaches, I command you to come out." I love this story!! In the name of Jesus who Paul preaches! Ha!

Verse 15 – 16 says this, "One day the evil spirit answered them, "Jesus I know, and Paul I know about, but who are you?" Then the man who had the evil spirit jumped on them and overpowered them all. He gave them such a beating that they ran out of the house naked and bleeding."

The response of the evil spirit makes me laugh! Jesus, we KNOW! Paul, we've **HEARD OF!** HA!! But who are you?? These demons recognised the name and authority of Jesus Christ – they had even heard of Paul – he had evidently become famous in the unhallowed halls of Hell. He had a reputation amongst the demons of the spirit world as **someone they knew about** – no doubt from experience.

So with my students from overseas, I would say, "Afraid the demons will jump me?? No not concerned at all because when I enter a temple, I'm sure the demons say to each other "Oh no it's Tom Rawls, we've heard of him, let's get out of here!"

I was never afraid of temples, never felt oppressed from entering a temple never experienced spiritual warfare after a visit to a temple. Once in Chaingmai, Thailand I slept right next door to a Thai Buddhist Temple and slept like a baby! I am not afraid of demons. I am not afraid of the dark either. On every encounter of demons, I was never afraid. I suppose I knew who I was in Christ and was always protected by a strong faith in the finished work of Jesus Christ!

In fact, I have never been afraid of evil spirits at all. I remember a night in Dhaka, Bangladesh when I was awoken at 2am. My room appeared to be really dark. No light was coming from outside at all. Within a few seconds, I became aware of a dark figure sitting on a chair in the corner of my room. I watched fascinated for about 10 seconds. I sat up in bed and pointed my finger at it said: "Go in Jesus name!" It vanished immediately. It was an evil spirit come to size me up, no doubt, and God had given me the opportunity to see and discern its presence. Fascinating!

Ephesians 6: 16 says, "In addition to all this, take up the shield of faith, with which you can extinguish all the flaming arrows of the evil one."

I love the way Paul speaks here – "In addition to all this" – take up the shield of faith! Don't take up just the belt of truth or the breastplate of righteousness but in addition to those things take up the shield of faith.

The power of doubt is great! We know how this has troubled our world and caused a great divide between many – not to mention that true truth is under assault by alternative truth. Satan's great weapon against us is his ability to deceive us and cause us to doubt.

His name is Deceiver because this is what he does so well. The enemy works against our own hearts and minds. His work centres on arguments and every pretension that sets itself up against the knowledge of God, and we are called upon to take captive every thought to make it obedient to Christ. If we don't, then strongholds can form in our minds, and we will fall in the evil day.

The enemy works with our weaknesses and manipulates our frailties to lead us into doubt. The battle is in our mind and emotions. The struggle is not flesh and blood but thoughts, desires, motivations and feelings. Because our hearts and minds can be deceitful, the enemy has a way in to work on us. It is for this reason we need the shield of faith.

The world system is a system infiltrated by the powers of darkness. The philosophies of the world system represent the world's views, ideas and values. And these ideas, inspired by darkness and motivated by sin, are then used by the enemy of our soul as weapons against us.

This is why Paul encourages us to be renewed in mind. **Romans 12: 2** "Do not conform to the pattern of this world, but be transformed by the renewing of your mind. Then you will be able to test and approve what God's will is—his good, pleasing and perfect will."

The Message Bible says it this way, "Don't become so well-adjusted to your culture that you fit into it without even thinking. Instead, fix your attention on God. You'll be changed from the inside out. Readily recognise what he wants from you, and quickly respond to it. Unlike the culture around you, always dragging you down to its level of immaturity, God brings the best out of you, develops well-formed maturity in you."

Listen to JB Philips Translation, "Don't let the world around you squeeze you into its own mould, but let God re-mould your minds from within, so that you may prove in practice that the plan of God for you is good, meets all his demands and moves towards the goal of true maturity."

One of the parts of the armour of God is a shield of faith "with which you can extinguish all the flaming arrows of the evil one."

What are the flaming arrows?
You've seen them in the movies – an arrow tipped with flammable material set on fire and shot from a bow. These flaming arrows hit a target and set fire to it. They are very dangerous and effective weapons of war.

Similarly, the enemy uses certain kinds of flammable thoughts, imaginations or pretentions as weapons. He fires them at us. It is as if these thoughts are like darts tipped with fire with this determination to inflame our imaginations.

These thoughts are incendiary and cause strong reactions within us – not just anger, but they ignite the worst passions, like fear, insecurity, flaming sexual desires, suspicion, cynicism, negativity, disappointment and disillusionment. These thoughts inflame natural feeling like unforgiveness, gossip or offence and turn them into forest fires out of control.

These are the furious and fiery suggestions of the enemy that incite evil and the excitement to sin! This is how the enemy works against you. This is where we are called upon by Paul to take up the shield of faith that can extinguish those fiery arrows.

The shield is the first barrier to an attack from the enemy. In Roman days the shield was oblong shaped and gave cover to the whole body. When a group of soldiers stand together, they each hold up a shield, and this manoeuvre is called "the tortoise." It is, in fact, a beautiful picture of the church in action too. Where we, as the church, offer protection for each other in a battle or a struggle.

It is a shield of faith.
Psalms 7:10 says, "My shield is God Most High, who saves the upright in heart."

The shield is all about our faith in God Himself – His nature, His character and our faith in Him. Faith in His revealed word. Faith in what He has done and will do on our behalf. Faith that He lives within us and will never leave us nor abandon us. We stand in faith knowing who God is. We stand in faith in the security of our salvation in Jesus Christ. The shield of faith is a firm belief in who God is. Faith in His love for us and that no one can be against us if God is for us. It is our first line of defence against the fiery arrows of the enemy!

Romans 8:31 says, "What, then, shall we say in response to these things? If God is for us, who can be against us?"

If God is for us, on our side, working with us and us working with Him then who or what can stand against us? The answer is nothing can stand against us – no person or thing can stand against us. It is the faith of patience and endurance, trusting in God's protection and submitting to His will, on which the darts of temptation, whether from fear, or from lust, or from doubt, fall harmlessly. It is with this faith we stand our ground against the enemy. His fiery darts fall harmlessly to the ground.

Romans 8:35 – 39 says, "Who shall separate us from the love of Christ? Shall trouble or hardship or persecution or famine or nakedness or danger or sword? As it is written: 'For your sake, we face death all day long; we are considered as sheep to be slaughtered.' No, in all these things we are more than conquerors through him who loved us. For I am convinced that neither death nor life, neither angels nor demons, neither the present nor the future, nor any powers, neither height nor depth, nor anything else in all creation, will be able to separate us from the love of God that is in Christ Jesus our Lord."

The shield guards our hearts and minds – this is the place the devil fires His flaming arrows. We need this faith in Christ as a protection to our lives. So we are protected by faith in who God is and what He has done for us. We stand in faith knowing we are "more than conquerors" through Jesus Christ. How great is our faith? It can quench the flaming arrows directed towards us by our enemy. Faith is the victory.

1 John 5:4 says, "This is the victory that has overcome the world, even our faith."

We stand in our faith in what He has done for us.
Forgiven – shame has been removed[12]
No condemnation – God is not angry with us, all of that anger was consumed by Christ on the cross.[13]
Justified – legally, just as if I had never sinned[14]
Healed – by His stripes I have been healed[15]
Free – the chains have fallen away[16]

Every curse has been broken[17]
He is with us and will never leave us[18]
He is more than enough[19]
I am a new person[20]
The enemy has been defeated[21]
On my behalf, Jesus died and rose again[22]

---

[12] Romans 10:11

[13] Romans 8:1

[14] Romans 5:1

[15] Isaiah 53:5

[16] Psalms 107:14, Galatians 5:1

[17] Galatians 3:13

[18] Hebrews 13:5

[19] Ephesians 1:3, 3:20

[20] 2 Corinthians 5:17

[21] Colossians 2:15, Romans 16:20

Temptation can be overcome[23]

Jesus defeated Death, Hell and Sin and rose again victorious over every work of darkness. Spiritual warfare is not about shouting to the Devil, binding him and rebuking him. No, the devil has no authority over us as we stand in our faith in Jesus Christ. Spiritual warfare is not a magical recital of words but a powerful immovable faith in Jesus Christ and His word.

1 John 5: 4 – 5 says "... for everyone born of God overcomes the world. This is the victory that has overcome the world, ***even our faith***. Who is it that overcomes the world? Only the one who believes that Jesus is the Son of God."

This is for everyone, not a few special ones, everyone, not a few favourites, but everyone, born of God finds victory. It's when we waver in our faith that we find ourselves losing the battle. It's when we waver in faith that we feel close to defeat. But as we stand strong and lift up our faith in Christ, the enemy finds little to no ground upon which to inflict a defeat! We win.

---

[22] 1 Corinthians 15:4

[23] 1 Corinthians 10:13

Chapter 7
The helmet of salvation

"And the questions they do ask are, of course, unanswerable; for they do not know the future, and what the future will depend very largely on just those choices which they now invoke the future to help them to make."
C.S. Lewis, "The Screwtape Letters"

"I think the devil doesn't exist, but man has created him, he has created him in his own image and likeness."
Fyodor Dostoevsky
A Russian novelist, short story writer, essayist, journalist and philosopher.

"For I am not ashamed of the gospel, because it is the power of God that brings salvation to everyone who believes"
Romans 1:16

In Thailand, there is a thing called a Sanphraphum – or a spirit house for the spirits of the land. It is a shrine found at the front of most houses in Thailand and found on most buildings including skyscrapers and department stores. The spirit house is there to house the spirits that protect the property and give the occupants good luck. These spirits need appeasing daily. The spirit house represents Thai's belief in a spirit world. They firmly believe in this realm of the spirit. This practice is not in accordance with the strict teaching of Buddhism, but is a manifestation of folk-fusion religious practice.

Inside the spirit house are two figures- an old woman and an old man. They represent the ancestors of the original owners of the land. They are given a sacrifice each day to appease them. These sacrifices are fruit and red Fanta or a red liquid. They do this each day and believe that in doing this, it gives them good luck and protects them from evil. No Thai needs to be convinced of the spirit realm. Paul also gives a startling and remarkable view of this realm in his letter to the Ephesians.

Ephesians 6: 16 says, "In addition to all this, take up the shield of faith, with which you can extinguish all the flaming arrows of the evil one. Take **the helmet of salvation** and the sword of the Spirit, which is the word of God."

The metaphor is obviously a Roman Soldier and his armour. Most people in Paul's time would be very familiar with a Roman soldier and what they looked like. Kids would know every aspect of the armour as they would play soldiers at home. My point is that Paul saw the armour as a whole, as a set, and yet for his instructions on spiritual warfare was able to identify each aspect with spiritual meaning and implications. He called it "God's Armour" and I think Paul would use it as a familiar sight to explain our position in Christ. I think Paul would preach on this metaphor regularly to rapt audiences.

In this chapter, I want to speak about the helmet of salvation. When a soldier was suited up for battle, the helmet was the last piece of armour to go on. It was the final act of readiness in preparation for combat. In fact, without the helmet, a soldier would be so vulnerable that the rest of the armour would be of little use. The helmet of salvation protects our mind. The breastplate protects the heart, the seat of our affections and emotions, but the helmet protects our mind.

- Our mind is the seat of our intellect, will, thinking, memory, perception and consciousness.
- Our mind gives a sense of subjective self-awareness.
- It is in our minds we carry out personal conversations with ourselves.
- Our mind is the seat of our imagination.

We can be of one mind or united in mind, you can be out of your mind, our minds can be set – it can be inflexible, determined or stubborn, we can be like-minded, we can be convinced in our minds of a truth, we can be double-minded, we can be mindful, we can change our minds and our minds can be probed by God's Holy Spirit. The mind is different from the heart, yet they are inextricably connected. Only the word of God can divide them.

Psalms 7:9 says, "… you, the righteous God who probes minds and hearts."

God can examine our minds – He can know our thoughts.

Psalms 26: 2 says, "Test me, Lord, and try me, examine my heart and my mind."

The Bible encourages us to be renewed in our mind. **Romans 12: 2** says, "Do not conform to the pattern of this world, but be transformed by the renewing of your mind." Our transformation is dependent upon us renewing our minds – to renew means to renovate, refurbish or restore to factory settings.

Our minds can be deceived. **Romans 16: 18** says, "By smooth talk and flattery they [from the context – people who cause division and put obstacles in our way – the religious rulers of the day] deceive the minds of naive people."

2 Corinthians 11:13 says, "But I am afraid that just as Eve was deceived by the serpent's cunning, *your minds may somehow be led astray* from your sincere and pure devotion to Christ." Note our minds can be led astray! We can be put off track or off course by the cunningness of the Devil.

2 Corinthians 4:4 says, "The god of this age has **blinded the minds of unbelievers** so that they cannot see the light of the gospel that displays the glory of Christ, who is the image of God." We can be blinded by demons.

Colossians 3:2 says, "***Set your minds*** on things above, not on earthly things." We can also set our minds. WE can adjust our minds, regulate our minds and align our minds.

William James, an American philosopher and psychologist, once said, "The greatest weapon against stress is our ability to choose one thought over another." Again he said, "The greatest discovery of my generation is that a human being can alter his life by altering his attitudes."

I think it is safe to say, our minds are a real target for the enemy. Remember, our mind is a spiritual entity. You can't pinpoint it on an anatomical chart. Our minds are subject to the tactics of the spiritual forces of evil. We have a faculty here which is enormously influential and controls much of our life and our behaviour. Is it any stretch that we need to protect our mind with a helmet of salvation specifically? It is with our hearts we feel, but it is with our minds we think. Both are a target of the enemy, and both need protecting.

This salvation which describes the helmet is our salvation in Jesus Christ. It is the free gift of God to all who believe.
- Salvation is all about restoring a relationship with God through Jesus Christ our Saviour.
- Salvation is forgiveness of sins, access by grace into God's presence forever.
- Salvation is the removal of guilt and shame and access to righteousness as a free gift.
- Salvation is a result of Jesus Christ's resurrection and victory over Satan, Hell, over death and over sin!
- Salvation means we are justified – legally just as if we'd never sinned.
- This is a position we have because of our salvation.

There are several actions a believer can take to keep this helmet fastened and functioning.

Proverbs 4:23 NCV says, "Be careful what you think because your thoughts run your life."

The helmet of salvation protects our mind. Our minds represent our psychology. It is what some say is our mind-set, *our thinking processes* and our consciousness. It can include our attitudes, our sense of right and wrong, which is our conscience-the part of us that determines right and wrong. Our minds inform us concerning our morality and help define our integrity. Our mind helps us to verbalise what we believe. The workings of our mind may, at first sight, be hidden but can, in fact, then play out over our faces. Micro-expressions can give away what we are thinking.

Renew our minds.
Our minds are battlefields. The outcomes of those battles determine the course of our lives. Protecting our mind is what the helmet of salvation does. That protection comes back to the word of God, our relationship with God and us understanding how God's principles work. Renew means to 'make it new again'. Returning our minds to God's factory settings. Renew is to renovate our minds;, refresh our minds. Fix the faulty hardwiring of our minds. We do this by allowing the word of God's truth to repair our mind's functions. Our minds have a habit of working in a particular way. We are called to renew the wiring. This process takes a while, but we will always have God's word to guide us. We will always have that confidence and security and assurance that we are His children.

Romans 12:1–2 instructs us to renew our minds by allowing the truth of God's Word to reprogram our thinking, to ensure it is in line with the truth of God's word. Old ideas, opinions, and worldviews need to be replaced. We must allow God's truth to continually wash away the world's philosophies, its lies, and confusion so we can adopt God's perspective. The reason we lose the battles of life is that we are so ignorant of God's word. We understand the Bible is an important book, but we find little to no motivation to pick it up and read it. Even less of a desire for it to inform us of what kind of life we should live.

1 Corinthians 2:16 says "But we have the mind of Christ." The helmet of salvation is our firm belief in the work of Jesus Christ on our behalf. Our faith in His word about who we are through the saving grace of Jesus. Having this helmet in place protects our thought processes and keeps us protected from the enemy's schemes and strategies that are designed to affect the way we think.

Doubt destroys our confidence. The enemy regularly comes to bring doubt into our minds. We see how he worked in the Garden of Eden when he said in **Genesis 3: 1**, "Now the snake was the most clever of all the wild animals the Lord God had made. One day the snake said to the woman, "Did God really say that you must not eat fruit from any tree in the garden?"

"Did God really say…? This has been a ploy of the enemy from the very beginnings of time. The devil schemes to foster doubt in your thinking about God, His word, His love for you, His salvation and His plan for your life. Doubt kills what God desires for you, but the helmet of salvation protects you from the power of doubt.

'Did God really say?' My response? Well let me check it out!

When we start to renew our minds in understanding and obeying God's word we are actually employing the helmet of salvation. The helmet protects our thinking by explaining salvation to our thoughts. I am secure in my knowledge of salvation no matter what the enemy would tell me, I know I am secure in Jesus. My salvation purchased by the death and resurrection of Jesus is sure and secure. I know what to think about Jesus and the way He purchased salvation for me.

Romans 5: 1 – 5 says, "Since we have been made right with God by our faith, we have peace with God. This happened through our Lord Jesus Christ, who through our faith has brought us into that blessing of God's grace that we now enjoy. And we are happy because of the hope we have of sharing God's glory. We also have joy with our troubles, because we know that these troubles produce patience. And patience produces character, and character produces hope. And this hope will never disappoint us."

This is how the helmet works. It reminds us of all the benefits of salvation. The helmet of salvation keeps my thought in the right place. My thoughts are renewed. I am who God says I am. I'm thinking in a godly way. We've been made right with God – there is nothing that can cause our disconnection! We have peace with God, even though the world around us swims with confusion, we have peace with God! I can't see my thoughts they are invisible. I can't see the enemy launching an attack against my mind either, it's invisible. But with the helmet, we can protect ourselves from this unseen realm.

We've been brought into the blessing of God's grace and have the confidence to come before His throne at any time. His grace is sufficient for us in our times of weakness. God is for me not against me. There is happiness and joy provided for us in times of sadness and grief. This is how the helmet of our salvation works to protect our thought processes, our minds and imaginations.

It's incredible how our imagination works. Within seconds we've imagined the worst things in the world. The doctor calls and asks for an appointment to see you, immediately we know we have cancer! The phone rings it's an unknown number immediately we imagine one of our children is hurt or missing. The helmet of salvation helps to protect us by keeping our imagination healthy and a creative force for good.

If something terrible has happened, we have the grace of God to keep us. Our faith in God is that when bad things happen, He's always there – so I need not fear the future. This is how the helmet of salvation works.

We need to remember that victory is already accomplished for us through our salvation, our union with Jesus Christ. When we understand the victory Christ won for us, we realise the enemy is a defeated foe and has no power over us. Yes, we need to be alert and aware, but we also need to know that our salvation purchased for us total and absolute victory over all the power of the enemy. It's that salvation that informs our minds about our victory and keeps us protected from the enemy's attacks.

1 John 4:4 says, "You, dear children, are from God and have overcome them because the one who is in you is greater than the one who is in the world."

This is why we sing and worship. This is why we love church. This is why we rejoice in the midst of hardship and trouble. Our God is able!

The more robust our understanding of what it means to be saved in Christ the greater our protection against the enemy. Knowing with assurance, 'I am saved', protects me and my mind, my imagination and my thought processes from the ploy of the enemy.
2 Timothy 2: 10 says, "Therefore I endure everything for the sake of the elect, that they too may obtain the salvation that is in Christ Jesus, with eternal glory."

Endurance is standing firm in the face of evil. Taking the helmet of salvation is our endurance – our stand in the evil day – this salvation that comes with eternal glory!

Chapter 8
The sword of the Spirit

"Hatred is best combined with Fear. Cowardice, alone of all the vices, is purely painful–horrible to anticipate, horrible to feel, horrible to remember; Hatred has its pleasures. It is therefore often the compensation by which a frightened man reimburses himself for the miseries of Fear. The more he fears, the more he will hate."
C.S. Lewis, "The Screwtape Letters"

"Those who play with the devil's toys will be brought by degrees to wield his sword."
Richard Buckminster Fuller
An American architect, systems theorist, author, designer, inventor and futurist.

"You believe that there is one God. Good! Even the demons believe that—and shudder."
James 2:19

An amazing account is found in the book of Luke chapter 4 when Jesus was being tempted by the Devil in the wilderness after fasting for 40 days! It appears the Devil came to Him while He was in a weakened moment. With no preamble, the Devil speaks to Jesus and says "If you are the Son of God turn the stones to bread."

A couple of obvious things. Doubt is being sown: "If" you are the Son of God. Then there was the temptation – turn the stones to bread. Jesus' response is classic. "It is written, man shall not live by bread alone."

Three times the Devil tempted Jesus and sought to sow doubt, but each time Jesus' response was the same. It is written. The Bible says! After three temptations the scripture says the Devil left Him. Unable to win the battle against Him. Here we find Jesus using the sword of the Spirit- the word of God! Amazing!

Ephesians 6: 17 says, "Take the... sword of the Spirit, which is the word of God."

Again, the analogy is of a Roman soldier's weaponry. Specifically, the sword. The sword used by Roman soldiers was known as a GLADIUS; and in the hands of a skilled man, it was a fearsome weapon. In fact, it became known as "the sword that conquered the world." It was sharpened on both sides, making it lethal against an unarmoured foe. The point was also sharpened, enabling it to pierce armour.

Now the gladius was used in battle against enemies which were flesh and blood – the sword was able to cut through armour as well as the flesh of men. Paul tells us though that this sword of the spirit is to be used in our struggle "against the rulers, against the authorities, against the powers of this dark world and against the spiritual forces of evil in the heavenly realms." The comparison of the sword of the Spirit to the gladius suggests it can do a bit of damage in the spirit realm, just as the gladius does damage in the natural realm.

I cannot emphasise enough, the passage of scripture in Ephesians 6 is remarkable in that it reveals to us that the war we fight is not natural – not flesh and blood – but spiritual. The struggles we experience take place in an invisible, unseen realm and it is inhabited by spiritual forces.

In the west, we relegate this "invisible realm" to nonsense or maybe just the stuff of TV shows. We love watching TV shows like "Salem" or "Outcast." We give this realm very little credence in our day to day lives and ignore it, to our detriment. We hear about evil spirits, occult practices or magic, and we believe that much of it is garbage and the rest is the work of charlatans. Yet within each of us is a certain place where there is fear of the darkness, the unknown or those things that "go bump in the night." There is a place where we know and understand the unseen, and it can scare us terribly.

In the west, we would prefer to be led by science, intellect and objective facts. We are so unaware of the unseen realm that we have relegated it to the fanciful or the fanatical. We've been taught not to see demons everywhere; as a result, we don't see them at all. I'm not endorsing crazy theology that gives the devil way too much airplay, but the neither am I endorsing taking the devil off the air entirely. Many do not even believe in the existence of the devil or even a spiritual realm. We do this to our detriment.

Charles Baudelaire, a 19th Century French poet in his book "Paris Spleen" once said, "The devil's finest trick is to persuade you that he does not exist."

Paul is however clear in Ephesians 6, "... be strong in the Lord and in his mighty power. Put on the full armour of God, so that you can take your stand against the devil's schemes." There is an enemy. He hates us and desires to destroy us, and he will use any and every scheme he can devise.

We know that very few of us would ever be significant enough to garner the actual Devil's attention as Jesus did in Luke 4. Satan is too busy working on people far more significant than us. But we are being targeted by what Paul refers to as 'spiritual forces of evil' which are active in the heavenly or unseen realms. So, what is the sword of the Spirit which is used in spiritual warfare? And how does it work?

1. It is a sword that belongs to the Holy Spirit and we are encouraged to "take it."
2. We are told it is a sword – an offensive and defensive weapon.
3. We are told it is the "Word of God."

A regular sword would be useless to us in fighting an unseen enemy, so we know Paul is speaking about something else. This sword, which is the property of the Holy Spirit, is called the Word of God. Now we know that words have great power – their power impacts us emotionally, intellectually but there is a psychological and cognitive response which has an unexplainable effect on us as a result of those mere words. Again, words have power. **Proverbs 12: 18** says, "The words of the reckless pierce like swords, but the tongue of the wise brings healing."

Solomon, author of the Book of Proverbs, regards words as having power. They can pierce like a sword. Words can harm you. But they can also bring healing. Words of encouragement are like that. We love them, and they nourish our souls.

Every one of us has had had people say nasty things to us, and we've been hurt. How do we protect ourselves from this kind of attack? How do we counter the attack of evil words against us? If words have this kind of effect, how much more so do the words of our enemy, the devil? Remember the enemy lies, he deceives and accuses us, and those words can smart or deeply cut us.

Remember the realm of the battle is the unseen. How do words hurt us? How do spoken words harm us? People can bring instruction, correction even say good things about us but the enemy has compromised us with our own insecurity, anxiety and fears, and what they say is not what we hear. As a pastor I've thought many times could I have said it differently? In the end though, I resign myself to the fact that even though I said something good it was their fear that turned into an accusation or a criticism.

Think about this for a moment: Our struggle is not against a thesaurus, but it is against an articulate, eloquent and intelligent enemy. The enemy is cunning and shrewd, he knows if he can compromise us in our self-identity he can twist other people's words to hurt us and further debilitate us.

Genesis 3: 1 – 5 says, "Now the serpent was *more crafty* than any of the wild animals the Lord God had made. He said to the woman, "Did God really say, 'You must not eat from any tree in the garden'?" The woman said to the serpent, "We may eat fruit from the trees in the garden, but God did say, 'You must not eat fruit from the tree that is in the middle of the garden, and you must not touch it, or you will die.'" "You will not certainly die," the serpent said to the woman. "For God knows that when you eat from it your eyes will be opened, and you will be like God, knowing good and evil."

Satan's voice and his word are real, and he uses it to bring doubt, to deceive and to lie to us. 'More crafty' means his voice is sensible, shrewd and perceptive; he sounds insightful and intelligent. His word is designed to bring doubt and uncertainty. His words are subtle and even underhanded. His words are designed to destroy us, so we must take great care in listening to this stuff. His word, is at its foundation, a lie. The Devil cannot speak truth, it just sounds like truth. The enemy's voice is smooth, charming, persuasive and slick: beware.

Proverbs 5: 3 – 4 says, "For the lips of the adulterous woman drip honey, and her speech is smoother than oil; but in the end, she is bitter as gall, sharp as a double-edged sword."

Note Eve's comments to the serpent: "God did say, 'You must not eat fruit from the tree that is in the middle of the garden, and you must not touch it, or you will die.'" She heard the command second hand from Adam. God never said they weren't to touch it, just not eat it (**Genesis 2:17**). In my experience as a pastor, I find there are many people with an incomplete knowledge of scripture and sometimes they actually make stuff up, just like Eve did. We really need to understand what the word of God actually says. We do this through a lifetime of studying it. We use it as the defence when the evil one comes with his dialogue.

Satan tempts us – he seeks to lure us, entice us and seduce us to act in a manner that is not in keeping with God's word. Satan's great playground is your mind! Let's look at the way Satan tempted Jesus in the wilderness after 40 days of fasting.

Luke 4: 1 – 13 says, "Jesus, full of the Holy Spirit, left the Jordan and was led by the Spirit into the wilderness, where for forty days he was tempted by the devil. He ate nothing during those days, and at the end of them, he was hungry. The devil said to him, "If you are the Son of God, tell this stone to become bread." Jesus answered, "It is written: 'Man shall not live on bread alone.'" The devil led him up to a high place and showed him in an instant all the kingdoms of the world. And he said to him, "I will give you all their authority and splendour; it has been given to me, and I can give it to anyone I want to. If you worship me, it will all be yours." Jesus answered, "It is written: 'Worship the Lord your God and serve him only.'" The devil led him to Jerusalem and had him stand on the highest point of the temple. "If you are the Son of God," he said, "throw yourself down from here. For it is written: '"He will command his angels concerning you to guard you carefully; they will lift you up in their hands so that you will not strike your foot against a stone.'" Jesus answered, "It is said: 'Do not put the Lord your God to the test.'" When the devil had finished all this tempting, he left him until an opportune time."

This passage gives us insights into how the sword of the Spirit works against the evil forces of darkness. When Satan comes to tempt us, or to speak to us, we counter him with skilful use of God's word. Jesus was protecting Himself from Satan's words by countering with God's word. Note the Devil knows scripture too – but he uses it against us. Amazing!

So, practically speaking the sword of the Spirit is our ability to use the word of God to counter the words of the enemy. This is a defence and protection against the false words of the enemy.

Think now about what you struggle with and where the struggle really is. Is it guilt, is it negativity or a lack of faith? Do you struggle with anger, lust, jealousy, and unforgiveness? Do you fight with anxiety, worry or fear? Do you get overly stressed? Are you tempted to sin? Are you confused, do you lack peace and hampered by a vague sense of doom? Do your thoughts sabotage you and debilitate you? We wield the sword of the Spirit in these occasions and counter the attack of the enemy with the word of God.

How does it work? This is not the only time the sword has been mentioned in scripture. Most notably in **Hebrews 4: 12 - 13**, "For the word of God is alive and active. Sharper than any double-edged sword, it penetrates even to dividing soul and spirit, joints and marrow; it judges the thoughts and attitudes of the heart. Nothing in all creation is hidden from God's sight. Everything is uncovered and laid bare before the eyes of him to whom we must give account."

God's word is alive and has the power to counter the lies of the enemy because His word is the truth. God's word is active – energetic, kinetic and dynamic – it has passion and is able to discern the negativity and falsehood of the enemy. There is a powerful and supernatural characteristic to God's word. God's truth, as it compares to the words of our enemy, clearly identifies the lie. It's in the comparison that we see the truth. God's word is the only objective source of truth to our spirit, it is only then we can counter the Devil's words to us.

God's word is sharp – contained within it is an incisive insight that cuts through the rubbish the enemy has been throwing at you. When the enemy speaks immediately, the Holy Spirit empowers God's word for our response. God's word is sharp – quick, intelligent, astute and clever – it so quickly illuminates falsehood and lies and emboldens truth. It's so sharp you begin to see things from a God perspective, instead of a human perspective. The enemy may be crafty, but God's word is sharp and incisive. The sword of the Spirit is like when you get a phone call from someone you don't know: they start to speak, and almost immediately you know this is a "cold call", and we can politely just hang up. In the same way, when the enemy speaks, God's word reveals the lie, and we just hang up because we know the truth lives with us.

God's word penetrates. God's word pierces the darkness of the enemy's lie with light. God's word penetrates lies with truth, penetrates deception with insight and penetrates trouble with hope! It penetrates because it is so sharp it cuts away the garbage and divides the rubbish from the real. It's so sharp it can peel the skin away from every lie.

God's word judges the thought and attitudes of our hearts, revealing them and exposing them to the light of God's truth. God's word is discerning, that means it is perceptive, judicious and discriminating. It can separate truth from error. This is how the sword of the Spirit works to protect us.

Nothing is hidden – nothing can be concealed – nothing is secret – nothing is hidden from view! All are exposed to God's eternal truth. God's word strips away the deception of the enemy's words about us. Everything is uncovered – every lie, every deceit, every untruth and every falsehood. God's word is light and exposes the darkness! To use the sword of the Spirit, we must be people who know the word of God.

Your ignorance of what God's word says, teaches and instructs us, could lead to your defeat in the day of evil. You must be a student of God's word. Read it. Meditate on it. Know it. If not, you will not be able to make a stand in the evil day. This is the reason we have so many weak Christians who fail to stand during their times of struggle. To stand and keep on standing we must know the word.

John 8:32 says, "You shall know the truth, and the truth will set you free." Know the truth, and that truth will set you free from the lies of your enemy. Imagine if you knew it well!

Imagine a life fed continuously upon the words of God's truth – imagine the health to your soul and mind, and your ability to stand in your evil day! Jesus is the word, and He expects us to be able to read and quote his word when we are in battles. When our mind is going crazy, we need to have an active and workable knowledge of God's word.

Chapter 9
Pray in the Spirit

"He sees as well as you do that courage is not simply one of the virtues, but the form of every virtue at the testing point, which means, at the point of highest reality. A chastity or honesty, or mercy, which yields to danger will be chaste or honest or merciful only on conditions."
C.S. Lewis,
"The Screwtape Letters"

"The potency of prayer hath subdued the strength of fire; it hath bridled the rage of lions, hushed anarchy to rest, extinguished wars, appeased the elements, expelled demons, burst the chains of death, expanded the gates of heaven, assuaged diseases, repelled frauds, rescued cities from destruction, stayed the sun in its course, and arrested the progress of the thunderbolt."
Saint John Chrysostom
Archbishop of Constantinople and was an important Early Church Father.

"For the eyes of the Lord are on the righteous and his ears are attentive to their prayer."
1 Peter 3:12

The spirit world is a mystery for many - the unknown, the uncharted country- especially for western Christians. In other parts of the world through people are not so unaware. Voodoo, witchcraft, magic, occult practices and the Dream Time this is the world of the unseen and believed in, so deeply, by others. These cultures value prayer and meditation and they are regarded as sacred. How much more mysterious is it when our Christian hearts pray to our Lord and God?

John Bunyan, English writer and Puritan preacher best remembered as the author of Pilgrim's Progress, ONCE SAID, "PRAYER IS A SHIELD TO THE SOUL, A SACRIFICE TO GOD, AND A SCOURGE FOR SATAN."

Samuel Chadwick, a Wesleyan Methodist preacher from the 1800's SAID, "PRAYER IS THE ACID TEST OF DEVOTION."

Williams Carey, a British missionary to India SAID, "PRAYER – SECRET, FERVENT, BELIEVING PRAYER – LIES AT THE ROOT OF ALL PERSONAL GODLINESS."

Brian Houston, global senior pastor of the Hillsong movement, recently tweeted on the 3rd July 2018, "Prayer is a weapon you can unleash against the devil, rendering him powerless."

IN **JOHN 17:5 JESUS** SAID, "My prayer is not that you take them out of the world but that you protect them from the evil one." Jesus prays for our protection.

Jesus said to his disciple, Peter, in **Luke 22: 31 – 32** TPT**,** "Peter, my dear friend, listen to what I'm about to tell you. Satan has demanded to come and sift you like wheat and test your faith. But I have prayed for you, Peter that you would stay faithful to me no matter what comes."

We are mostly ignorant of the unseen because we only believe in what we can see and the unseen is the unknown. We wonder why we must pray. We wonder if our prayers work. We lack an understanding of the dynamic behind the power of our prayers. Yet the Bible teaches us that there is an unseen world, populated by evil forces of darkness that are solidly against us and prayer is a powerful weapon against them.

This Ephesians passage speaks about God's armour and is explicit in the descriptions. I have covered all six of the pieces of a Roman's soldier armour. I want to speak about the last piece that Paul mentions. He breaks from the Roman armour metaphor, but this last piece of our armour is no less potent! Paul calls us to pray in the Spirit.

Ephesians 6: 18 – 20 says, "And pray in the Spirit on all occasions with all kinds of prayers and requests. With this in mind, be alert and always keep on praying for all the Lord's people. Pray also for me, that whenever I speak, words may be given me so that I will fearlessly make known the mystery of the gospel, for which I am an ambassador in chains. Pray that I may declare it fearlessly, as I should."

Take up the whole armour of God AND pray in the Spirit! Potent advice from the author.

Your secret weapon – praying in the spirit.
The baptism in the Holy Spirit was the "promise of the Father" in **Luke 24: 49**. The 'clothing in power' spoken of in **Acts 1**. Jesus said it would empower us to go to the four corners of the globe for the service we would perform for Him. Jesus promised to not leave us as orphans in **John 14: 18** but He would give us the Holy Spirit, another just like Him.

Jesus spoke to his disciples very clearly about waiting in Jerusalem until they had received power from Heaven. **Acts 1: 4 – 5** says, "He gave them this command: "Do not leave Jerusalem, but wait for the gift my Father promised, which you have heard me speak about. For John baptised with water, but in a few days you will be baptised with the Holy Spirit."

Further to Jesus' instruction, He said in **Acts 1: 8** "But you will receive power when the Holy Spirit comes on you, and you will be my witnesses in Jerusalem, and in all Judea and Samaria, and to the ends of the earth." **Acts 2** is that story and day one of the promised power that was to clothe us.

One of the main benefits of baptism in the Spirit is, not only explosive energy that would empower our lives but, a gift to be able to pray in tongues as our holy prayer language. Scripture refers to this as "praying in the spirit." Here in Ephesians 6, Paul concludes his teaching about God's armour with an instruction to pray in the spirit.

Jude 20 says, "… build yourself up in your most holy faith and pray in the Holy Spirit."
1 Corinthians 14: 14 – 15 says, "For if I pray in a tongue, my spirit prays…"

Romans 8: 26 – 27 says, "We do not know what we ought to pray for, but the Spirit Himself intercedes for us."

Pray in the Spirit on all occasions. This is written in the context of spiritual warfare. So is this time to shout and bind the demons in Jesus name? I think not. We are told to pray all kinds of prayers and make requests, but we are also advised to pray and "be alert and always keep on praying."

I think, at times, our prayer can be focused on breaking strongholds and declaring the victory of Jesus over situations and circumstances. But again be alert. Be always attentive, watchful and vigilant. Don't lose your focus. Jesus is Lord and has delivered to us a stunning victory over all the powers of darkness. Our prayer is one of declaring this stunning victory. Being alert and praying for wisdom and insights as we stand in the evil day. Prayer in the Spirit secures our victory, our wisdom and our insight.

We are encouraged to pray for God's people as well. Remember this was a time of great persecution for the church. Many of God's people were being killed for His namesake. Families were being split up, church gatherings were being targeted, and Rome's power and might was coming against them.

2 Timothy 2: 1 – 3 says, "I urge, then, first of all, that petitions, prayers, intercession and thanksgiving be made for all people for kings and all those in authority, that we may live peaceful and quiet lives in all godliness and holiness. This is good, and pleases God our Saviour."

Paul encouraged God's people to pray for the governing authorities not because they were necessarily good – not even to make them good - but that they, the church, might "... live peaceful and quiet lives in all godliness and holiness." Even in the midst of a bloody reign by Roman leaders, Paul says our struggles are spiritual. So pray in the Spirit for our governments. Embolden yourself, be empowered and edify yourself by praying in the Spirit.

So pray in the Spirit. Be full of the Spirit. Overflow with the power of the Holy Spirit. Build yourself up in the Holy Spirit. This is how we protect ourselves from the schemes of the Devil. It is through prayer we find ourselves drawing close to God and seeing the Devil flee. Prayer is an excellent part of the armour of God, and it is one we would do well to apply to our lives.

I wish I could give you some extraordinary revelations about prayer, but prayer is uncomplicated and straightforward. The subject matter of prayer may be difficult. We often times need to speak to God about our weaknesses and troubles. The good news is the access we have in prayer is simple and assured. We speak to God – it is a conversation. We speak and then listen for Him to speak. I don't understand why people are so lethargic and idle in prayer. It is a powerhouse. God hears our every prayer and moves Heaven to reach us in our times of need. We pray, and God speaks. We need to listen as well. You listen by bowing your knees with a copy of His word in your hand.

In recent days, I have been meditating on the passage in **Genesis 32** when Jacob wrestled with God. I have often times felt like this. It is a wrestling, a struggle and I cannot sleep because I am so fervent in my prayers. God is well up for us fighting together in prayer. Making our request known to Him. At times prayer is about describing our disappointment to Him. God's up for us talking straight to Him and asking those hard questions which should not be uttered! I mean there have been times as I wrestle with Him that I am very very blunt with Him and ask why He hasn't fulfilled His word to me! In prayer, I have allowed my disappointments to bubble up and I find myself speaking in a very direct manner to Him. I'm sure there are some angel that blush, but I need real answers from God. These are tough times of prayer. This is praying in every occasion! But God is up for it and at the end, as He did with Jacob, He will bless us.

Take care you don't allow circumstances to speak to you. Circumstances are not always God speaking to you. They are mostly difficult times we will all have to go through. God is with us and will never leave us to battle alone. On many occasions, it will be the Lord who fights for us. In our struggles and wrestling, we will always need God's understanding as we walk through life – we will need His perspective- and we will need the Holy Spirit to interpret circumstances for us. Just because you're in a tough time doesn't mean God has abandoned you.

Prayer opens us up to revelation.
Prayer allows us to come up to God and see things from His perspective.
Prayer brings revelation and understanding.
Our prayer in the Spirit is powerful and protects us in the day of evil. Paul asked and so do I, "Pray also for me, that whenever I speak, words may be given me so that I will fearlessly make known the mystery of the gospel, for

which I am an ambassador in chains. Pray that I may declare it fearlessly, as I should."

Epilogue

There's no denying it. We will all face our days of evil. We will all experience tribulation and trial. We are all going to have tests, tough times and difficulties. It's all about how we navigate them that makes all the difference.

In the early church, they faced martyrdom, our struggles are not nearly so "life and death" as theirs, not in the western church anyway! But our struggles are no less real and distressing. How we cope is vital. How we face these trials is essential. We need to be armed with a good understanding of the source of our distress.

It's true many of us experience distress because of the consequences of our sin or just bad decision making. **John Wayne,** TV cowboy and movie star, once said, "Life's tough, especially if you're stupid!" We can never underestimate the power of bad decisions. Bad decisions seem to be the kick-off point for bad luck, circumstances that seem to spiral out of our control and a turmoil that explodes our comfort and peace.

So wisdom is paramount in our decision making. Having insight and understanding of what will happen if we do this or that. But an essential ingredient to good decision making is our integrity and character. If we are people who have a God honed sense of right and wrong, we are more likely to make better decisions. The results that come from bad decisions is not then us railing against evil spirits but of coming before our gracious God in repentance seeking grace in times of need.

Our decisions affect people too. How we treat people, and this is a decision of our heart, is important. Paul says we don't wrestle against "flesh and blood", but there are times our lack of wisdom and integrity impact other people's lives, and it is then we need grace, wisdom and humility to make a situation right. We salvage a relationship when we act in integrity, expressing godly sorrow when we mistakenly see flesh and blood as the source of our struggle. There are times we need to apologise to people, and do it with humility and with integrity.

If our lives are rooted and growing in the soil of righteousness, then we will live lives worthy of His name. We will live like a letter from heaven and people will respect us and respond well towards us. If we decided to act out of a sense of sinfulness, then our actions will negatively impact people as well, and we'll need the wisdom to repair those broken or fractured relationships. What got us into these dark moments of trial was a bad decision, what gets us out is integrity, honesty and a desire to do right towards our neighbour.

Even when we act badly by making stupid decisions, there is no guarantee the enemy will not seek to capitalise on our misfortune. In fact, our misfortune becomes a staging ground for the enemy to attack, leveraging our own stupidity against us. There are human beings we need to consider. Some we may need to apologise to and humbly ask for forgiveness. Others we may need to humble ourselves and seek reconciliation with them. In the midst of a natural situation, we face the enemy and his relentless hostility directed against us. Often times it is our spiritual response that prepares the way for us to reconcile with those we have hurt or offended.

Now if you murder someone, you will be judged and go to jail. No doubt. I hope they do judge you and you do go to jail. We need to get dangerous people off the streets. In the midst of this, the enemy will have a field day complicating your already complicated situation. The consequences of some bad decisions will result in judgement and sentencing. Some of our decisions will only stain our lives, where as other will ruin our lives. The magnitude of your decisions and choices will vary, and the level of judgement and condemnation will also vary, but do not be ignorant the enemy will work overtime to complicate an already bad situation.

It is, for this reason, we are to develop integrity and work on our character to avoid these costly damages to our way of life.

Proverbs 19:3 NLT is clear "People ruin their lives by their own foolishness and then are angry at the LORD." We need to stop blaming the Lord or blaming the devil and begin to grow by taking responsibility for our own action, choice and decisions. This is not spiritual warfare this is spiritual growth and discipleship. We can't say, "The Devil made me do it" just as we can't say, "God allowed this to happen."

Bad things happen to stupid people because of their stupidity not because of a devil or demon. They chose. They decided. They did it. Now we are all subject to temptations, but consequences are a result of our choices and actions based upon our integrity and righteous, not the temptation.

1 Corinthians 10:13 TPT says, "We all experience times of testing, which is normal for every human being. But God will be faithful to you. He will screen and filter the severity, nature, and timing of every test or trial you face so that you can bear it. And each test is an opportunity to trust him more, for along with every trial God has provided for you a way of escape that will bring you out of it victoriously."

The consequences for doing right is blessing. The consequence for doing wrong is judgement – not by God either but by those we have sinned against; governments or individuals. It is so clear in scripture!

Galatians 6: 7 – 8 says, "Do not be deceived: God cannot be mocked. A man reaps what he sows. Whoever sows to please their flesh, from the flesh will reap destruction; whoever sows to please the Spirit, from the Spirit will reap eternal life."

There is no doubt the enemy capitalises on our decisions and can make things worse. However we need to do business with God first, deal with governing authorities and individuals we offended and fight the unseen war second. We need to rescue our integrity which we lost through a lack of wisdom. We need godly discipline to be disciples of Jesus. Then we can stand in our evil day even if we were the force that caused it all.

The Devil will use every device in his arsenal to seek our defeat and ultimate destruction. He will use every ploy, scheme and strategy to overthrow us. But we have no need to make it easy for him though, by a lack of integrity. As we mature and exercise more responsibility, we have a responsibility to close the gaps in our margins of error and walk in wisdom.

God will always be our shield! He has promised that. He has promised to make us strong in our weaknesses and to deliver us from the evil one. God has promised never to leave us or abandon us to enemy's devices. God loves us and desires to protect and cover us every moment and every day of our lives.

But it becomes imperative we walk wisely.

1 Thessalonians 5: 6 – 8 says, "So then, let us not be like others, who are asleep, but let us be awake and sober. For those who sleep, sleep at night, and those who get drunk, get drunk at night. But since we belong to the day, let us be sober, putting on faith and love as a breastplate, and the hope of salvation as a helmet."

How we walk is our choice. We can walk in the light, as He is in the light, or we can walk in darkness. We can live our lives motivated by the light or tempted by the dark. The choice is yours.

Paul encourages us to be awake and sober. Awake - to watch, be alert, attentive, prepared and vigilant. Sober - clear-headed, restrained and not under the influence of something that would make us thoughtless, careless or reckless. So Paul instructs us to be sober and to "put on faith and love as a breastplate, and the hope of salvation as a helmet."

There is a remarkable connection here to the Ephesians scripture. Now we know that 1 Thessalonians was one of the earliest New Testament books written, so it's not a stretch that, like every good preacher, Paul expounded on this thought and, nearly 25 years later, wrote to the Ephesian church to teach about the armour of God.

But please note for all those who scream at demons and see demons everywhere. Paul encouraged us to be awake and sober, motivated by the righteous light of God's heart and His word. To live and walk in the light, putting on faith and living by it. To put on love as a breastplate and walk in love. To put on the hope of our salvation, like a helmet to protect our minds, in this grand battle against our enemy. Our enemy is a totally and utterly defeated foe. He is a foe never the less, but we have victory over him.

In our salvation, God has accomplished so much! We've been rescued from the dominion of darkness, no longer under Satan's control or manipulation. We've been translated or supernaturally moved into a new relationship with a new King. We are now under the righteous rule of Jesus Christ. We've become new creations, because Jesus now lives within us. Jesus has defeated the old regime, and we are now under a new governmental body led by the Lord of all the earth, Jesus Christ. We've been born again, and now we can see the kingdom of God. Satan's power over us has once and for all been broken. We've been set free from Satan's power and are free to love and serve Jesus Christ.

Hebrews 2:14 – 15 says, "Since the children have flesh and blood, he too shared in their humanity so that by his death he might break the power of him who holds the power of death-that is, the devil and free those who all their lives were held in slavery by their fear of death."

In giving us salvation, Jesus has broken the power of the Devil over us and given us freedom. We've been rescued from this present evil age. The Devil's power over you has been broken! His power over you has been shattered, ruined and destroyed. He no longer has any power over you. You are free in the life Jesus has provided for you.

Galatians 1: 3 – 4 says, "Grace and peace to you from God our Father and the Lord Jesus Christ, who gave himself for our sins to rescue us from the present evil age, according to the will of our God and Father." We've been rescued. It was a staggering and earth-shattering rescue. It has been proclaimed for everyone who believes in Jesus Christ. We have a new King. A King who no longer holds us as captives but as His family, His friends, who bow before Him, not because we are forced to, but because of our love for Him.

Colossians 2: 13 - 15 says, "When you were dead in your sins and in the uncircumcision of your flesh, God made you alive with Christ. He forgave us all our sins having cancelled the charge of our legal indebtedness, which stood against us and condemned us; he has taken it away, nailing it to the cross. And having disarmed the powers and authorities, he made a public spectacle of them, triumphing over them by the cross."

We need to know this and have it as foundational understanding about how great our salvation really is! We were once dead in sin, but God made us alive with Christ. What the Holy Spirit did with Jesus, He has done with us; we've been raised to new life because of our belief in Jesus Christ. Just like the resurrection, we too have been quickened by the Holy Spirit to new life and with new allegiance.

In our salvation, we've been forgiven all our sins and, through Jesus, God has now cancelled the legal charges against us, our debt has been paid by Jesus Christ on the cross, and the purchase price was His precious blood! As a result, those charges levelled against us have been taken away. The condemnation which hung over us as a deadly diagnosis has been nailed to the cross of Jesus. Jesus took it all away when He saved us - when we believed on Him. And for each of us, Jesus has now presently, at this very moment and from the moment He died and rose again until today, Jesus has disarmed Satan and all of his demons who are working actively against us. Jesus has disarmed them and has made a public spectacle of them.

These demons have now become the laughing stock of the unseen realm. Jesus humiliated their master Satan and made a public spectacle of him and every demonic force in step with him. It wasn't a private affair, no, it was a very public affair. Every angel is heaven has witnessed it, all of the universe beheld it, and to those who are being saved, we too have seen this public spectacle. Jesus has triumphed over them all through the cross. Such amazing and awesome news for those of us who seek to stand in the evil day!

I hope and pray the emphasis of this book will not escape you. Simple and yet profound. A life lived in His service is protection enough from the beggarly element of a ragtag team of broken and defeated spirits. Don't get me wrong, they are enraged, angry and hostile towards us, but Jesus has made a public spectacle of them and has given us victory over every last one of them.

In the closing words of this book, my prayer is that we put on God's armour and seek to walk with integrity in the righteousness of Christ. To do this as a daily discipline. In doing so, we will continually blunt the enemy's attacks against us, giving him no foothold or wedge into our lives.

I pray we will live passionately, always ready to share our story about Jesus, knowing that the very message of salvation is powerful beyond measure, bringing forgiveness to every repentant soul.

I pray we will be a people who walk in faith, a strong faith in God's eternal word. As we do so, we will deflect every arrow aimed at us.

I pray we walk with a full and experiential understanding of our salvation, knowing what Jesus did for us, what He purchased for us and what He accomplished for us. May we know the power of new life, quickened by the Holy Spirit daily, as we move forward as the indomitable church of Jesus Christ.

I pray that you will be empowered by the word of God, emboldened by the word of God and supercharged by the word of God. I pray that you will wield this sword of the Holy Spirit to give life and set them free from darkness, to assure people of their victory and to encourage them to live a life worthy of Jesus Christ.

I pray you will pray! Pray always in the Spirit, being built up, edified and made strong. May you pray in the Spirit without ceasing, praying the mind of the Spirit when you lack your own words and direction to pray!

Here, my fellow pilgrims, is a toast to victory over the realm of darkness! Be blessed and live well.

Tom Rawls, August 2018

Acknowledgements

Nobody does this alone. So I would like to thank a few of people for editing, reading and commenting on 'Unseen'.

Thanks to Sam Cousins and Scott McCrum for creating the cover artwork.

Thanks to Tim Handley for proof reading, page setting and publishing advice.

Thanks to Laura Miles for proof reading and her wonderful advice and comments.

Thanks to Amy Calow for editing and proof reading.

Thanks to the people of Proclaimers for being people of such great faith and commitment. I feel so honoured to be your pastor.

Finally, thanks to my amazing wife, Denise, for her enduring support.

We have provided these pages for you to make your own notes as you explore *Unseen*.